INSIDE
the
DATABASE
OBJECT
MODEL

Donald K. Burleson

CRC Press

Boca Raton   Boston   London   New York   Washington, D.C.

Library of Congress Cataloging-in-Publication Data

Burleson, Donald K.
   Inside the database object model/Donald K. Burleson.
      p.   cm.
   Includes bibliographical references and index.
   ISBN 0-8493-1807-6
   1. Object-oriented databases.   I. Title.
QA76.9.D3B8745   1998
005.75'7—dc21   98-6349
                                                                         CIP

No claim to original U.S. Government works
International Standard Book Number 0-8493-1807-6
Library of Congress Card Number 98-6349
Printed in the United States of America 1 2 3 4 5 6 7 8 9 0
Printed on acid-free paper

Dedication

To my wife Janet, whose love and kindness has transformed my life.

If a man can write a better book,
preach a better sermon,
or make a better mouse-trap,
than his neighbor,
though he build his house in the woods,
the world will make a beaten path to his door.

Ralph Waldo Emerson
A Thousand and One Epigrams (1911)

Contents

Preface

The long march away from relational databases and into database objects has not been smooth. This transition has presented a hugely confusing plethora of approaches and techniques, with each database vendor touting their own unique approaches to the introduction of objects. However, one thing is clear; virtually ever major database vendor has recognized the benefits of Object Technology, and they are all introducing object-oriented features into their database products. Unfortunately, it is ironic that a technology that promises to simplify database development has suffered a bad reputation as a confusing and complex paradigm. Terms like polymorphism, inheritance, encapsulation, and the obtuse syntax of the object-oriented languages have all fostered an aura of mystery, and many mainstream database developers remain blissfully unaware of Object Technology in the vain hope that the paradigm will fall from favor.

Object-orientation has been a buzz word for nearly a decade, but it is only recently that the major players in the database market have made a commitment to using the principles and techniques of object-orientation into their products. To confound this transition, most of the major relational architectures are not ideally suited to support database objects, and the database professionals must wade through a distressing amount of technical jargon and poorly explained techniques.

It is now abundantly clear that database objects are going to play a major role in the future of data processing, and professionals everywhere are struggling to embrace this new way of processing information.

The purpose of this book is to explore the nature of database objects and to explain in plain English how object technology is going to change the face of the mainstream relational database engines. Regardless of the differences in vendor implementations, the database object model remains firm in its' goal of introducing reusable data objects that can communicate seamlessly across database architectures and platforms.

This text will begin by providing a generic understanding of the tents of object technology, exploring each of the salient features of objects and describing how they apply to the database object model. We then move on to describe how database objects are incorporated into mainstream databases, and describe all of the relational database extensions that are being introduced to create database objects. Finally, this text will take a look at the emerging standards for database objects and examine how the major database vendors are working to achieve their goals.

I believe that the compelling benefits of database objects are going to drive this technology into the mainstream. I also believe that the that the transition between traditional relational database processing and object technology will be very painful. Hopefully, this text will help the reader to clear up their confusion about database objects and understand how objects are being incorporated into virtually every aspect of database processing.

Don Burleson
Raleigh, North Carolina

The Author

During the 1980s, Donald Burleson established himself as a national expert in database architectures. A popular speaker and author, Don has published more than 50 articles in database management in national publications, and remains a regular contributor to all of the national periodicals, including *Computerworld*, *DBMS Magazine*, and *Database Programming & Design*. Don is an accomplished and entertaining speaker who has taught more than 100 college courses. He has served on the faculties of several large universities, including the University of New Mexico, Webster University, Empire State College, and the Rochester Institute of Technology. Don is the author of seven books on database design, including: *Practical Application of Object-oriented Techniques to Relational Databases*, *Managing Distributed Databases*, *High-performance Oracle Applications*, *Using Oracle on the Web*, *High Performance Oracle Data Warehousing*, and *High-Performance Oracle8 Tuning*.

Acknowledgments

Special thanks to Rick and Joanne Tytler for their assistance in the preparation of the manuscript.

1

The History and Evolution of Object Technology

Database management systems have come a long way from the primitive file management systems of the 1960s. As each successive database generation was introduced, improvements in functionality led to a progression whereby each succeeding database generation contained major improvements over the preceding generation. As seen in Figure 1.1, the hierarchical model brought us the ability to establish relationships between data items, the network database brought us the ability to model complex data relationships, the relational model brought us declarative data access, and the object-oriented database brings us the coupling of data with the behavior of the data.

The next database generation is clearly moving toward the incorporation of object-oriented functionality into the database engine. With the properties of encapsulation, abstraction, and polymorphism, object technology is moving toward a unified data model which models the real-world far more effectively than possible in any of the previous database systems. Furthermore, a properly designed object-oriented data model promises to dramatically improve the maintenance process. This is because all changes to data attributes and behaviors become a database task, within the controlled boundaries of the database management system (DBMS), and changes are no longer made to external application programs.

Presently, the relational model is the most popular and widely used vehicle for database systems. This popularity of the relational model is attributed primarily to its innate flexibility and the ease of use that accompanies SQL. However, the relational model has been with us for more than a dozen years, which is an extremely long time for any computer architecture. To appreciate the old-age of relational systems, look back ten years to the state-of-the-art technology of the 1980s. Today, it would be ridiculous to use a decades old product such as the CPM operating system or the Visicalc spreadsheet, yet we continue to rely on database models that were developed decades ago.

Customers are no longer satisfied with the shortcomings of relational databases and the relational model needs to be updated to handle the increasingly demanding requirements of the data processing community. For example, existing relational databases do not support repeating groups within tables and they require that all data is modeled at its smallest level. Any data item

1

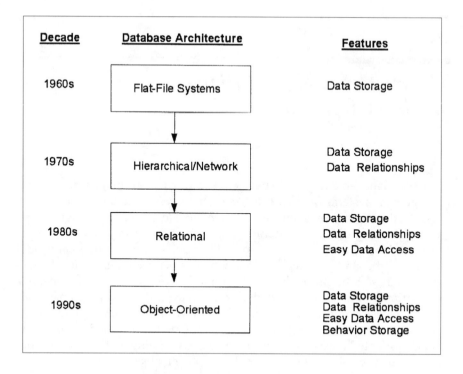

Figure 1.1   The evolution of database technology.

that does not consist of atomic table data must be recreated at run-time with a view each time that it is referenced.

Just as structured programming languages like Pascal were first introduced to enforce structured programming techniques, object-oriented databases enforce the coupling of data with behavior. Furthermore, the object data model is designed to be flexible and can handle the changing business needs of dynamic organizations.

Many professionals have been scared away by all of the obtuse jargon and incomprehensible C++ code that is usually associated with Object Technology. Furthermore, the idea of an "object paradigm" has served to make mainstream database professionals wary of this new technology. Fortunately, the reality of Object Technology is very different from this perception. When properly presented, object-oriented database development is a natural extension of the structured programming approach that has been used for decades. Indeed, there are many parallels to Object Technology in the history of procedural languages. Just as structured programming emphasized the benefits of properly nested loop structures, object-oriented development emphasizes the benefits of modular and reusable computer code, and the benefits of modeling real-world objects. In short, database objects will soon become a *de facto* standard for all information systems.

The object-oriented technology approach started because certain specialized applications required robust features that could not use traditional programming languages like Cobol or Fortran. In these environments, the complexity of the processing and the complexity of the data relaionships were beyond the capabilities of traditional database engines. Today, Object Technology remains very popular in complex data processing environments such as the telecommunications industry.

However, we would be remiss if we led the reader to believe that object orientation is a panacea for all of the ills that have plagued the computer industry. While the object database model has some very compelling features, there is a downside. The greatest hinderance to Object Technology is that object data models are very rigid and inflexible when compared to relational databases, especially when the data model is being designed. Unlike the ad hoc nature of relational database development where data items can easily be added to a model and new tables can be quickly joined to existing tables, object-oriented systems require careful up-front planning, especially within the class hierarchies. However, with careful planning, an object data model can be just as robust as a relational database, and in some cases superior, since inheritance and overloading can be used to quickly modify an existing database.

Object-oriented systems are most widely noted for their ability to achieve maintenance requests quickly by adding new classes to the class hierarchy, but this ease of maintenance does not come without a price. In order to achieve the promise of low maintenance, these systems need to be very well defined before coding begins, and the analysis phase of object-oriented systems development may take far longer than an analysis of a traditional system.

Unfortunately, object-oriented database development is a very foreign concept for many relational database professionals. Object orientation is a new paradigm, and object orientation requires a new way of looking at the storage and retrieval of data.

While it is indeed true that object-oriented languages such as C++ and SmallTalk have a very steep learning curve, the programmers who have mastered them may be many times more productive than those using traditional languages. However, the object-oriented approach is only 5% technology and 95% philosophy. In many cases, once the programmers are trained to think in object-oriented technology terms, they find that existing procedural languages can be used to accomplish many of the tasks which were once thought to be exclusively for C++ and SmallTalk. For example, many object-oriented technology features such as fully reentrant procedures and reusable code can be implemented with a classic language such as Cobol.

One of the main goals of object-oriented database technology is increasing productivity and the useful life of the database. Organizations that are willing to undertake the learning curve associated with object-oriented technology have found tremendous benefits, both in reduced development efforts as well as less ongoing maintenance costs. Figure 1.2 shows costs and time for object-oriented versus Cobol systems development.

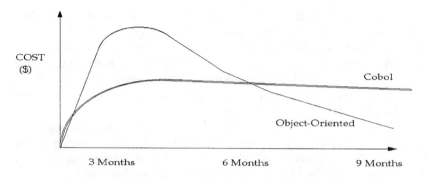

Figure 1.2   Development costs as a function of time.

In object parlance, the storing of an object on disk is called "object persistence," and this process generally involves taking an in-memory object and creating an exact copy on disk storage. Just as a relational row will exist in memory (in the database buffer) and on disk, an object will exist in memory and will have a parallel structure on disk. This idea of parallel objects on disk and memory presented a real challenge for early object-oriented database developers. Lacking a database management system, many programmers using C++ and SmallTalk store their own complex objects in a file system of their own design. These "home grown" databases are generally linked-list data structures which serve to store the objects, but they do not take advantage of the inherent benefits of a database management system. Today, most systems professionals realize that it is possible to incorporate object-oriented functionality into existing relational database software, and some vendors are developing object-oriented front-ends for relational databases.

Basic Principles of Object Technology

There has been a huge difference in the evolution of hardware and software in the industry. Hardware advances are a routine matter of course, while we continue to use procedural languages that were developed decades ago. Today, computer hardware continues to increase in power and speed at a phenomenal rate. Software, on the other hand, remains very difficult to develop and maintain. Often, the problems with software development originate with the systems-analysis phase of development. As we know, the job of a systems analysts is to gather the logical requirements for a new system, or to define the changes to an existing computer system. The tools of the systems analyst are very well defined and generally include data-flow diagrams, a data dictionary, and process logic specifications. The systems analysis methods have also been around for decades and are showing their age. By the same token, the systems analysis methodologies that were developed by Gane & Sarson, Tom DeMarco, and Ed Yourdon were developed at a time when systems were not incorporating many of the advanced features of object orientation. Structured analysis concepts such as functional decomposition, top-down design, and data-flow diagrams are used in their analysis. The analyst gathers and documents the system requirements and then asks the client to sign-off on the specs. Essentially, the end user must approve the analysis saying this is what they want, while the analyst is saying that this is what will be delivered.

Unfortunately, the traditional development approach is not ideally suited to object-oriented analysis. This is because the complex nature of database objects and the mapping of the object to the behavior of the object are inherently complex and unknown to the end users of the system. Hence, a wealth of new approaches to object-oriented analysis have emerged. The industry has been presented with object-oriented analysis methodologies by Jim Rumbaugh, Grady Booch, Ed Yourdon, Peter Coad, and a host of other theoreticians. While all of these methodologies share some common goals, their permutations are very complicated, leaving many Information Systems developers confused and bewildered. As of 1998, no single approach has achieved enough inertia to become a de facto standard, and many object database developers choose their methodology by using the methodology that is supported in their object CASE tool.

Another shortcoming of traditional system development methods is that they fail to plan for changing functional requirements. The business world today is changing at an unprecedented rate and computer systems need to be able to change as quickly as the business needs of the organization. It has become a historical reality that most computer system projects today seldom are done on time or completed within their budget. Furthermore, when the project is finished it can be extremely difficult and expensive (if not impossible) to make updates to the system. What is needed is a new approach to developing computer systems, one that can handle both small and large systems and can handle a dynamic environment where the system continually changes. Maintenance costs must be kept to a minimum, the system must be designed for flexibility. In practice, those companies that have been successful with object technology keep this fact a closely guarded secret. Their ability to react quickly to a changing environment is a huge competitive advantage, and one that they are not willing to share. In sum, object-oriented information systems have allowed companies to "turn on a dime," quickly changing their databases to meet changes in external requirements.

To achieve this lofty goal of flexible databases, we must first break out of the software paradigm that has been around for the last fifty years. The best thing that has happened in this change is the commitment of the major relational vendors to add object capability to their databases. As companies are forced to look at object databases, object-oriented technology will help to break the existing software paradigm and allow developers to create databases that are infinitely flexible.

As we have noted, the numerous problems with traditional systems development have led to a movement to find a better way to create and maintain database systems. The next evolution of database design appears to be the object-oriented technology method, and virtually all of the major database vendors have promised object features. Object-oriented databases will not only store data, the relationships between data, but they will also couple the behavior of the data with the data itself. Once the behaviors (called "methods" in object parlance) are added into a database management system, these "intelligent" databases promise to dramatically change the development of database systems.

The Object Technology (Object-Oriented Technology) method not only uses the intelligent database concept but enhances it by adding additional features. Instead of simple database triggers that are associated with a physical event such as the insertion of a row, object-oriented methods may contain operations which affect hundreds of database objects. Objects are "encapsulated" with their methods, and as a result no data items may be accessed or updated except through these methods. Of course, this object-oriented principle of encapsulation violates the relational database concept of data independence. In the relational model, data and process are deliberately independent and SQL may be used to access any data, anywhere in the database. Unfortunately, any type of "ad hoc" data access is prohibited in the Object Technology model. This is a major problem with coexistence strategies for relational databases and object-oriented databases, and is fully addressed in Chapter 10, "Interfacing an Object-Oriented Application with a Relational Database."

It is important to understand that object technology has been with us since the late 1980s and has enjoyed only limited acceptance in the marketplace. One of the reasons that Object Technology has languished in the backwaters is the lack of standards, the high learning curve, the nascent tools, and the inflexible nature of the "pure" object databases. However, all of this is going to change when all of the major database vendors embrace the object approach.

We see the same problems with object databases that we saw with the early relational database offerings. Each Object Technology database vendor, impatient with the lack of standards, seems to be doing their own thing, implementing Object Technology according to their own needs and requirements with very little thought about interoperability with other vendors. In an attempt to address this lack of standards, a consortium of Object Technology vendors got together and formed the Object Management Group, commonly called the OMG. The purpose of OMG is setting standards for object technology, and their first set of specifications were released in 1993. OMG and other object-setting standards groups will be covered in detail in Chapter 4, "An Overview of Object Database Standards."

One of the most confusing things about Object Technology is all of the new terms, jargon, and acronyms. Every new technology has its share of buzzwords—the "OO" acronyms were becoming a laughingstock in the industry. Some of the early OO acronyms included:

OOPS	Object-oriented programming systems
POOP	Principles of object-oriented programming
FOOD	Functional object-oriented development
OOA	Object-oriented analysis
OOD	Object-oriented design
MOOSE	Multi-faceted object-oriented systems engineering
GOOD	Generalized object-oriented development
OODBMS	Object-oriented database management system

In addition, several organizations emerged:

SOOPA	Symposium on Object-Oriented Applications
ECOOP	European Conference on Object-Oriented Programming
OOPSLA	Object-Oriented Systems and Languages Association

During the early 1980s, object orientation become the "oat bran" of the computer industry, with every vendor claiming to have it, but with no real definition of object orientation. To put an end to this plethora of acronyms, the OMG decided to rename object orientation as Object Technology or Object-Oriented Technology.

Since that time a whole new list of Object Technology acronyms have cropped up:

OMG	Object Management Group
ODMG	Object Database Management Group
CORBA	Common Object Request Broker Architecture
OMT	Object Modeling Technique
UML	Unified Modeling Language

The History of Object-Oriented Programming Languages

Beginning with modeling languages such as SIMULA, many object-oriented programming languages (OOPL) have evolved and have been incorporated into object-oriented database systems. In their 1993 specifications OMG endorsed C++ and SmallTalk. For programming to be considered object oriented it must use encapsulation, inheritance, and polymorphism.

C++ has emerged as the most dominant object-oriented language. C++ is really an extension of C language which is not object oriented in nature. Object technology purists will be quick to point out that C++ is not a pure object-oriented language, and as anyone who uses C++ will tell you it is very difficult to learn and master. C++ actually got its name from the C programming language, where the double plus sign (++) is used to add a variable, and since C++ is the next extension of C, the ++ was added to the name.

Incrementing a Counter

```
Cobol:    add 1 to counter
Basic:    counter = counter + 1
C:        counter++
```

SmallTalk, on the other hand, is a pure object-oriented language which makes the programmer follow the Object Technology methodology. Small-Talk is easier to learn than C++ and because of its nature, most colleges and universities have endorsed it as the standard teaching language. Most students learn SmallTalk as their first object language and then move on to learn other OOPLs.

Basic Object Oriented Features

In the fifteen years since the introduction of object orientation, there remains a wide variance in the definition of Object Technology. If the industry cannot agree on the common definition of an object, then it makes sense that the industry has been unable to reach a consensus on the features that comprise object orientation.

Database objects are no exception. An object-oriented database must contain some basic object architecture properties in order to be considered a database object, but a debate remains about exactly which features are required. For example, an Oracle8 database object does not support inheritance, but is regarded as an object nonetheless.

We see the same kinds of issues surrounding support for multiple inheritance in programming languages. For example, in the object-oriented language SmallTalk, multiple inheritance is not supported, even though multiple inheritance is considered to be a part of the object architecture. The following section explores the general features of object technology and explains the basic precepts of the object model.

Classes

A class is defined to an object database much as a schema is defined to a relational database. Just as a row in a table can be said to be a row in a "customer" table, a database object can be said to be an object of the "customer" class. In essence, a class characterizes one or more objects that have common methods,

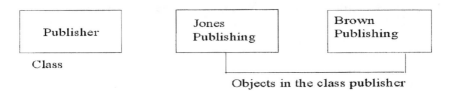

Figure 1.3 The difference between a class and objects within the class.

variables, and relationships (Figure 1.3). Here we see that that "Publisher" is the class name, while "Jones Publishing" and "Brown Publishing" are objects within this class definition.

Whenever a class contains identifiable subclasses, the classes may be defined to the database as a hierarchy. This means that a "general" class can be broken down into other more specific classes. In a class hierarchy, a "base" class serves as the anchor for the class hierarchy, and the base class contains all data structures and methods that are common to all class definitions in the hierarchy. From the base class, we diverge into more specific classes. A member class is commonly referred to as a subclass, while the owner class is called a superclass. A subclass can also be decomposed where it, in turn, becomes the superclass for all classes below it. On the other hand, a superclass can be thought of as a combination of all of its' subclasses. If you combine the subclasses you would form a superclass as shown in Figure 1.4.

In Figure 1.4, we see that the vehicle is the superclass and automobile, boat, and airplane would be defined as subclasses. As we have noted, classes serve as the templates from which specific objects are created. They serve as the "blueprint" to "stamp out" objects when they are created. A class contains

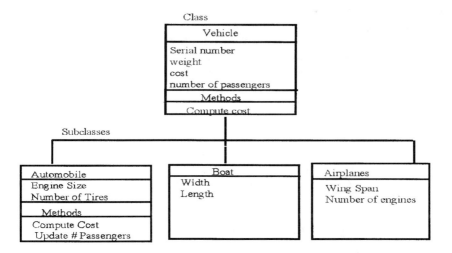

Figure 1.4 An example class hierarchy.

attributes (sometimes called variables), and these attributes are combined from all participating superclasses to become the data definition part of the object when it is created. When defined in a class definition, attributes describe the class; when an object is created, these descriptions become variables.

In addition to data definitions, classes also contain the behaviors (methods) that can be applied to the variables inside an object. The method definitions remain in the class definition, ready to be called by database objects.

In Figure 1.4 we see that the VEHICLE class definition contains numerous data attributes including serial number, weight, cost, and number of passengers. The class AUTOMOBILE has the data attributes of engine size and number of tires, The BOAT class has the data attributes width and length, and AIRPLANE has the data attributes wingspan and number of engines.

The methods for a class define the set of operations that can be performed upon an object. For example, when a method is applied to an object it will either return a value or the method will perform some operation to update the values in an object. As seen in Figure 1.4, a method for VEHICLE might be used to compute the cost of the vehicle, returning the dollar value of the vehicle. Sometimes methods do not return values. If a method was designed to update the number of passengers for a vehicle, no value would be returned but a data item inside the target object would change value.

Database Objects

Objects are the fundamental concept in an object-oriented database. In essence, objects are an abstract representation of real-world things that are stored in an object-oriented database. An object is an instance of a class, in the sense that it is stamped out from the class definition. The object contains all the data structures from its class definition as well as the data structures from all of its super classes (via inheritance).

The methods are stored with the class definition, and the objects know how to access the class definition so that they can be used to perform their functions on the data in the object. One of the features of the "pure" database object model states that data in an object can only be accessed by using one of the objects methods, but many object/relational vendors have ignored this requirement.

When we say that an object is an instance of a class, we mean that all objects of the same class contain the same data items, but each data item may contains different values (Figure 1.5.)

In concrete terms, you can think of an object as a self-contained package that has three parts:

1. Its own private information (data values).
2. Its own private procedures that will manipulate the objects data values. (via the class definition).

3. A public interface so that this object can communicate with other objects.

An important point about objects to remember is that objects are created from their object class, and they know their class through an Object Technology principle known as *strong typing*. They share all of the data structures and methods with their class and are tightly bound to their class definition. In this way, a class definition becomes a data type and we can create pointer data types that must match the object. For example, if we defined a data element as containing a pointer to an automobile, a pointer to a ship may not be inserted into this element.

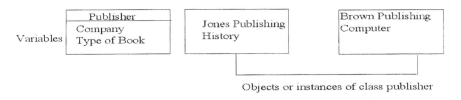

Objects or instances of class publisher

Figure 1.5   An object with values.

Within most object databases, objects are given a system-generated unique identity when they are created, called the Object Identifier (OID). Unlike a relational database where a row in a table is free to exist without a primary key, the object model requires that each object has a system-wide unique address. OIDs are explained in Chapter 2, but basically the OID that is assigned to an object stays with the object for the life of the object and will never be reused, even after the object has been deleted. The OID is always unique and no matter what object methods are applied to the values inside the object, the OID will never change. One thing that an OID lets us do is distinguish between two or more objects. Using the OID we can determine if two objects are equal, that is, if two objects contain the same values.

Comparing Classes and Objects

Many neophytes confuse the terms class and object and often use the terms as if they were interchangeable. In the real world, a class (or class hierarchy) is the definition that hold the data structures and methods for objects. Hence, a class is used to initially create a database object (a term called instantiation), and when a method for an object is invoked. In other words, a class can be thought of a the "rubber stamp" from which individual objects are created. Let's summarize our discussion of objects and classes:

Classes

- A class is a template for a group of objects.
- A class is a definition with common variables and methods.
- Classes are hierarchical in nature.
- Classes can have subclasses.
- Classes are sometimes referred to as an object type.

Objects

- An object is an instance of a class.
- Each object is given a unique object identifier when it is created.
- When an object is created it "inherits" all data attributes from the class definition.
- When a method is requested against an object, it inherits all methods from it's class and its superclasses.
- Each object has its own private data storage area in memory.
- Each object has public interfaces.

In Object Technology the terms "object" and "class" are often used interchangeably. Sometimes the term object is used to refer to a class and other times object is used to mean an instance of a class. Remember, objects are an instance of a class but they also contain all of the properties of the class that created them.

Messages

Messages are how programmers activate the methods for an object, and they are very similar in form to the stored procedures and functions that we see in relational databases except that they are tightly coupled to their object class. There are two distinct forms for methods—the procedure method and a function method. A procedure method never returns a value, but may updates values within objects, while a function method will always return a value. A message can tell an object to perform virtually any type of operation. A message will either update some of the objects data or perform some calculation and return a value to the calling program. Generally speaking, a parameter string is associated with the message, and this parameter string includes all of the necessary input and output definitions (Figure 1.6.)

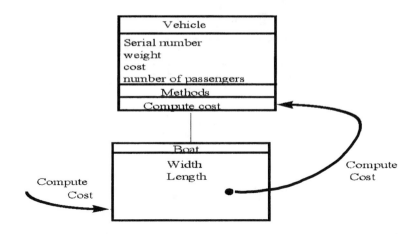

Figure 1.6   Messages being sent to objects.

Here are some examples of message calls to database objects:

```
order_total = compute_order_total(123);
    /* This returns an integer */
credit_status = check_customer_credit("jones");
    /* This returns a Boolean */
Update_inventory_level("widget", 37373);
    /* This does not not return a value */
```

The message with the parameter string being sent must match one of the object's interface types (methods) in order to perform the requested operation. If the method cannot be found in the class hierarchy then an error will occur.

Messages in Object Technology are very similar to subroutine calls in conventional programming languages. Conventional languages would have one procedure call another procedure, which, in turn, may call other procedures, and so on. For example, the calling procedure (sender) would ask another procedure (receiver) for some information, the sender would send a parameter string with the call and the receiver would send the requested information back to the sender using the parameter string.

Abstract Classes

It is critical to the understanding of class definitions to note that not all class definitions we use will be called to create objects. The top levels in a class hierarchy are seldom instantiated and are called abstract classes. An abstract class is a class that serves only to pass data structures and methods to lower level classes when they are instantiated.

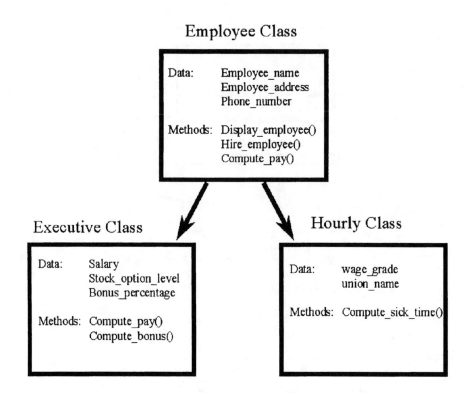

Figure 1.7   Abstract class.

An abstract class can serve a very useful purpose with inheritance. When each subclass is used to create an object, the object inherits all of the data structures associated with the abstract class. At runtime, the abstract class definitions are used for the inheritance of methods, via the Object Technology principle called "late binding."

Now that we understand the basic concepts behind the definition of a class hierarchy, let's take a look at the definitions for encapsulation and abstract data types within the database object model.

Encapsulation and Abstract Data Types

Unlike the relational database model that requires all table columns to be defined from fixed data types such as NUMBER and VARCHAR, the Object Technology model provides support for user-defined data types. This is true of both the pure object databases as well as the object/relational database engines.

For example, commonly used aggregations of base data types could be defined and reused within the database. Consider the following example:

```
CREATE  TYPE  full_address  (
    street_address  VARCHAR(30),
    city_name       VARCHAR(30),
    state_name      CHAR(2),
    zip_code        NUMBER(%));
```

We are now free to use this data type in the definition of a database object:

```
CREATE  TABLE  customer  AS  OBJECT  (
    customer_name     VARCHAR(200),
    customer_address  full_address);
```

Given this definition, all instances of the customer objects will use the full_address data type and create a data structure as shown in our definition. Here we can also see a shortcoming of the Object Technology model. To illustrate, what happens when we need to change the size of zip_code from 5 digits to 9 digits? Most object/relational implementations allow for the ALTER TYPE syntax to change the class definition, but we must be able to deal with restructuring the objects that already exist in the database. Hence, modification to a data types, especially those that appear high in the class hierarchy, may require special utilities to visit each database object, and restructure them.

Let's start by looking at traditional programming languages and their built-in data types. Traditional languages are based on text and numerical data types, and you are limited to the kinds of data types that the programming language will support. Variables that are used by the programming language have to be defined using one of the supported data types. Object Technology has done away with the restrictions of just using these built in data types and allows you to create different data types. Once these new data types are defined they are treated the same way as built in data types. The ability to create new data types when needed and then use these data types is called "data abstraction," and the new data types are called abstract data types (ADTs).

Just like a class definition, an abstract data type is more than a set of data values. When defined, some Object Technology databases allow for methods to be used along with the data definition. Returning to our previous example, a full_address data type could be defined so that it only contained street_address and zip_code. A method could then be associated with the full_address data type to use the value of the zip_code to retrieve the city_name and state_name from a set of lookup tables.

Data abstraction and ADTs are a cornerstone for Object Technology because they can be created as needed, and this helps you to think of and design computer systems to more accurately reflect the way data types are represented in the real world.

One of the main reasons why hierarchical, network and relational databases are being replaced is their failure to support ADTs. These traditional databases have very strict rules foe the layout of data and simply are not flexible enough to handle ADTs.

Encapsulation and Database Objects

Encapsulation gathers the data and methods of an object and puts them into a package, creating a well-defined boundary around the object. Encapsulation is often referred to as "information hiding," and encapsulation can be used to restrict which users and what operations can be performed against the data inside the object.

Classes provide encapsulation or information hiding by access control. A class will grant or deny access to its objects using the public and private access specifiers. Public members define an interface between a class and the users of that class and public members can be accessed by any function in a program. Objects can contain both public and private variables: the public variables are used with the objects methods or interfaces and the private variables are only known to the object and cannot be accessed by an interface. For example, a private method might be used to compute an internal value, and the calling method would not be aware of the private method of any of the variables that were used by the private method.

Encapsulation can be used in non-database object-oriented applications to guarantee that all operations are done via the methods that the programmer has defined in the class definition, insuring that data can not be changed outside of its own predefined methods. However, declarative database languages such as SQL allows for what might be called "declarative" retrieval and updates of data, and does not follow the rules of encapsulation. This is called an impedance mismatch, and is inconsistent with object-oriented database management.

As an example, in a relational database we could define a behavior called ADD_ORDER which will check to see if there is enough product in inventory for the order. The order object will not be created if there was not enough product in inventory. This behavior will make sure that no order is placed for product that is unavailable. However in a relational database, you could use SQL and bypass this validity check and thereby add an invalid order into the database.

Inheritance and Database Objects

Two of the benefits of Object Technology are code reusability and extensibility, and inheritance allows the implementation of both of these features.

When new objects are created they can inherit the data attributes or variables from their class and all classes above them in the class hierarchy. Because a method is procedural code, when an object inherits methods, it also inherits the programming code associated with the method.

Inheritance is a very powerful concept, but it is also an easy concept to understand. When a class is broken down into another class or classes, the class that was broken down is called the superclass and the resulting class or classes are called subclasses. These subclasses then inherit all of the methods and variables of the superclass.

To illustrate inheritance, consider the following example. In Figure 1.8, a JET object would inherit all variables from the AIRPLANE class, including wingspan and number of engines data fields. In addition, the JET object would inherit all of the variables from the VEHICLE class, including serial number, weight, cost, and number of passengers.

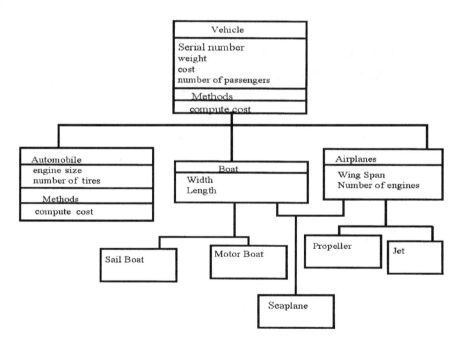

Figure 1.8 A sample inheritance hierarchy.

There are two types of inheritance in Object Technology—single inheritance and multiple inheritance. Single inheritance means that a subclass has only one superclass, while multiple inheritance allows a subclass to have more than one superclass. Up to now we have discussed only single inheritance. Multiple inheritance is a very complicated concept that is not very well understood. Some object-oriented languages such as SmallTalk do not support multiple inheritance. In Figure 1.8, if we were to add a SEAPLANE class, it would be part boat and part airplane, so it would inherit methods and variables from both the BOAT and AIRPLANE class.

Some object/relational databases do not support inheritance, but the products have promised to implement inheritance in future releases. More on this later in this chapter.

When a method is requested, there are two ways that the method can be delivered. With late binding, the databases will start at the class definition, and move up the class hierarchy until the method is found. With early binding, the programmers specifies the class where the method is located. The use of early binding will disable method inheritance, since the object will not search the class hierarchy.

Important Facts about Inheritance

It is critical to the understanding of inheritance to note that inheritance happens at different times during the life of an object.

1. **Inheritance of Data Structures**—At object creation time, inheritance is the mechanism whereby the initial data structure for the object is created. It is critical to note that only data structures are inherited—never data. It is a common misconception that data is inherited, such that an order may inherit the data items for the customer that placed the order. We must understand that inheritance is only used to create the initial, empty data structures for the object. In our example, all vehicles would inherit data definitions in the vehicle class, while an object of a lower-level class (sailboat) would inherit data structures that only apply to sailboats—as in sail_size.

2. **Inheritance of Methods**—Inheritance also happens at runtime when a call to a method (stored procedure) is made. For example, assume that the following call is made to sailboat object:

```
SAILBOAT.compute_rental_charges();
```

The database will first search for the **compute_rental_charges** in the sailboat class; if it is not found, the database will search up the class hierarchy until **compute_rental_charges** is located.

Polymorphism and Database Objects

Polymorphism is the ability of different objects to receive the same message and respond in different ways. Polymorphism simplifies the communication between objects by using a common interface to hide different implementation details. Polymorphism adds a high degree of flexibility to Object Technology by allowing new objects to be added to a computer system without modifying existing procedures, helping to reduce maintenance, and allowing systems to change more rapidly as customer needs change.

As an example of how the same message can have different behaviors, think of the event PROMOTION at work, this event will have different behaviors based on the class of EMPLOYEE that receives the promotion. A MANAGEMENT option might receive stock options and a bonus, but a PROGRAMMER object might receive a new title called senior programmer and a 2% raise.

Polymorphism was a spin-off of a programming concept called "overloading." Overloading is basically the ability of a programming method to perform more than one kind of operation depending upon the context in which the method is used. A very simple example of this is the use of the operator "+", in working with characters it can be used for concatenation and if used with numerical values it would be used for addition. A programming example would look as follows:

Concatenation example:

```
First_Name = "Janet"
Last_Name = "Lavender"
Full_Name = First_Name + Last_Name
```

Numerical example:

```
Counter = Counter + 1
```

In Figure 1.8, both classes AUTOMOBILE, and VEHICLE have a method called compute_cost. The process of having different classes with identically named methods is called method overloading. For example, if we wanted to compute the cost of an automobile the method in the AUTOMOBILE class would do the calculation. However for boats and airplanes the cost would be computed in the VEHICLE class. The reason for putting a compute cost in the AUTOMOBILE class is that the calculations are different for a boat than for an airplane.

Extensibility

Extensibility is an especially powerful concept that allows an object-oriented database to handle novel data situations easily. Extensibility is the ability of an object-oriented system to add new behaviors to an existing system without changing the application shell.

For example, consider a database called customer. The database has pre-existing definitions of the CUSTOMER class and also has two defined objects within this class, called NEW_CUSTOMER, and NORMAL_CUSTOMER.

Let's assume that we want to create a new object, FAVORED_CUSTOMER. An object-oriented database would allow us to create a new class definition, specifying the unique data attributes of this class, and creating the behaviors for FAVORED_CUSTOMER(s). Once defined, FAVORED_CUSTOMER objects can be created and referenced in the same fashion as any other objects within the database schema.

Benefits of the Object Technology Approach

As we have seen, object-oriented databases make the promise of reduced maintenance, code reusability, real-world modeling, and improved reliability and flexibility. However, these are just promises, and in the real world some users find that the object-oriented benefits are not as compelling as they originally believed. For example, what is code reusability? Some will say that they can reuse much of the object-oriented code that is created for a system, but many say there is no more code reusability in object-oriented systems than in traditional systems. Code reusability is a subjective thing, and depends heavily on how the system is defined. The object-oriented approach does give the ability to reduce some of the major expenses associated with systems, such as maintenance and development of programming code. Following are some of the benefits of the object-oriented approach:

1. **Reduced maintenance**—The primary goal of object-oriented development is the assurance that the system will enjoy a longer life while having far smaller maintenance costs. Because most of the processes within the system are encapsulated and reside inside the database engine, the behaviors may be reused and incorporated into new behaviors in an ad hoc fashion. Also, the ability to extend an existing class hierarchy means that the object database can be quickly extended to handle new classes of objects with the guarantee that these extensions will not effect any existing objects in the database.

2. **Real-world modeling**—Object-oriented systems tend to model the real world in a more complete fashion than do relational database methods. Objects are organized into classes of objects, and objects are associated with behaviors. The model is based on objects, rather than on data and processing, and real-world objects can be directly represented without having to create a relational view.

3. **Improved reliability and flexibility**—Object-oriented systems promise to be far more reliable than traditional systems, primarily because new behaviors can be "built" from existing objects. Because objects can be dynamically called and accessed, new objects may be created at any time. The new objects may inherit data attributes from one, or many other objects. Behaviors may be inherited from superclasses, and novel behaviors may be added without effecting existing systems functions.

4. **High code reusability**—When a new object is created, it will automatically inherit the data attributes and characteristics of the class from which it was spawned. The new object will also inherit the data and behaviors from all superclasses in which it participates. When a user creates a new type of a widget, the new object behaves "wigitty", while having new behaviors which are defined to the system.

The Current State of Object Technology

There has been a huge debate about the benefits of adding objects into mainstream database management. For years, a small, but highly vocal group of object-oriented bigots preached the object revolution with an almost religious fervor. However, the object-oriented databases languished in the backwaters until the major relational database vendors made a commitment to incorporate objects into their relational engines. Now that object-orientation is becoming a reality, systems developers are struggling to understand how the new object extensions are going to change their lives.

There are many varying definitions relating to object orientation, and each vendor will come up with their own justification for their implementation of Object Technology. For example, Microsoft has stated that it does not feel that support for inheritance is required in order for a product to be called object oriented, and they continue to pronounce OLE 2.0 as object oriented despite this shortcoming. In the database arena we see the same thing. Oracle version 8.0 also does not support inheritance although they have promised this functionality in a future release. Regardless, Oracle8 is being marketed as a relational/object database engine.

The Use of Java with Database Objects

The Java language became popular in 1997 with the widespread interest in extending the world wide web. Java is an object-oriented procedural language, but like most other object-oriented languages, Java does not support

pointers for linking objects together. Hence, it is impossible to use Java as a
sophisticated data vehicle, since Java objects cannot be linked to establish any
relationships between objects. Regardless, Java holds great potential as a language that can be used to extend the functionality of existing database servers. In terms of syntax, Java is best described as "C++ without pointers."

The Informix Object Model

As we have discussed earlier, Informix purchased the Illustra database
engine with an eye toward melding it with their Informix online relational
database. While other vendors such as Oracle provide database tools for
many platforms, Informix has remained firmly entrenched in the UNIX
arena. In fact the name Informix is a derivative for INFORMation/unIX, and
one of the strengths of Informix in the Unix market was their use of an architecture that was specifically tailored for use in a Unix environment.

The Oracle Object/Relational Database Architecture—
A Closer Look

While the standards are emerging for database objects, we are seeing a wide
diversity of opinion about the best way to implement the database architecture.

In 1996, virtually all of the major relational database vendors made a commitment to add object support into their engines. Their implementation of
objects, however, has been very different. Oracle originally committed to
rewrite their engine to become object oriented, but later changed their
approach, and extended their relational architecture. Informix, on the other
hand, purchased the Illustra object-oriented database and undertook to create a new hybrid of Illustra with their relational engine.

In general, the Oracle8 object/relational engine is remarkably similar to
the relational engine found inside the relational Oracle, but with major
extensions to the relational architecture and the addition of table and index
partitioning. It is interesting to note that Oracle has not discarded the idea
of creating a "universal" database engine. In fact, Oracle is calling Oracle8
the *Oracle Universal Server*, adding text and multidimensional and object
capabilities to the relational engine. In addition to object support, the
enhancements involve the introduction of a text search engine (ConText),
and the incorporation of the Oracle Express multidimensional database. But
most importantly, Oracle version 8 has coupled an object layer with the relational engine.

The Oracle8 model, however has fallen short of the features that are found in a "pure" object-oriented database. Oracle8 has been able to introduce the following features:

1. Abstract data types (user-defined types)
2. Introduction of object IDs
3. Establishing data relationships with OIDs
4. Building aggregate objects with OIDs
5. Allowing repeating groups within objects
6. Coupling objects with behavior (methods)

However, Oracle8 has not introduced support for class hierarchies, and the associated inheritance and polymorphism that come from classes, although Oracle claims to be planning for this functionality in later releases. In short, Oracle's commitment to objects was not just acknowledgment of a fad; the benefits of being able to support objects is very real, and the exciting new extensions of Oracle8 are going to create the new foundation for database systems of the 21st century.

When glancing at the Oracle8 documentation, these extensions seem very mundane. These new features essentially consist of user-defined data types, pointers to rows, and the ability to couple data with behavior using methods. However, these new additions are anything but mundane. They are going to change the way that databases are designed, implemented and used in ways that Oracle developers have not been able to imagine.

Oracle database designers will no longer need to model their applications at their most atomic levels. The new "pointer" construct of Oracle8 will allow for the creation of aggregate objects, and it will no longer be necessary to create Oracle "views" to see composite objects. Relational databases need to be directly able to represent the real world. The object-oriented advocates argued that it does not make sense to dismantle you car when you arrive at home each night, only to re-assemble your car every time that you want to drive it. In Oracle7 we must assemble aggregates using SQL joins every time that we want to see them. Finally, relational designers will be able to model the real-world at all levels of aggregation and not just at the third normal form level.

This ability to prebuild real-world objects will allow the Oracle designer to model the world as it exists, without having to recreate objects from their pieces each time they are needed. These real-world objects also have ramifications for Oracle's SQL. Rather than having to join numerous tables together to create an aggregate object, the object will have an independent existence, even if it is composed entirely of pieces from atomic tables (Figure 1.9).

This modeling ability also implies a whole new type of database access. Rather than having to use SQL, Oracle8 databases may be "navigated", going

Objects are composed of many database entities.

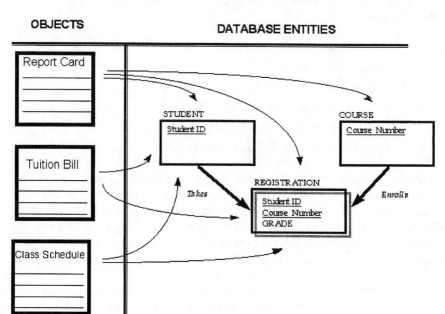

Figure 1.9 Objects are made up of atomic relational entities.

from row to row, chasing the pointer references without ever having to join tables together. Navigational data access will allow Oracle designers to create faster links between tables, avoiding some of the time-consuming SQL join operations that plague some systems.

Finally, the ability of Oracle8 to tightly couple data and behavior will change everything. Rather than having all of your process logic in external programs, the process code will move into the Oracle database, and the Oracle engine will manage both the data and the processes that operate on the data. These "methods" were first introduced into the object-oriented model to provide encapsulation and reusability. Encapsulation refers to the requirement that all data inside an object can only be modified by invoking one of its methods. By having these pretested and reliable methods associated with the object, an Oracle object "knows" how to behave and the methods will always function in the same manner regardless of the target objects. Reusability is achieved by eliminating the "code hunt". Before methods were introduced, an Oracle programmer would have to scan through Pro*C programs or stored procedures searching for the code that they desired. With methods, the developer only needs to know the name of the class associated with the object, and the list of methods can easily be displayed. The availability of these reusable methods will change the role of the Oracle programmer from being code craftsmen. Just as the introduction of reusable parts changed the way American manufacturing functioned, the introduction of reusable code will change the way that Oracle systems are constructed and maintained.

However, this reusability does not come without a price. The structure of the aggregate objects must be carefully defined, and the Oracle developer must give careful thought to the methods that are associated with objects at each level of aggregation. Libraries of reusable code will develop to be used within new Oracle systems.

Now that we have seen the compelling benefits of object/relational databases, let's take a closer look at how Oracle8 has implemented these features. Oracle has implemented the object/relational model in stages, introducing objects in Oracle 8.0 and inheritance in Oracle 8.2.

Oracle User-Defined Data Types

The ability of Oracle to support user-defined data types (sometimes called abstract data types, or ADTs) has profound implications for Oracle design and implementation. User-defined data types will allow the database designer to:

1. **Create aggregate data types.** These are data types that contain other data types. For example a type called full_address could contain all of the sub-fields necessary for a complete mailing address.

2. **Nesting of user-defined data types.** Data types can be placed within other user-defined data types to create data structures that can be easily re-used within Oracle tables and PL/SQL. For example, a data type called customer could be defined that contains a data type called customer_demographics, which in-turn contains a data type called job_history, and so on.

Pointers and Oracle

One of the new user-defined data types in the object-relational model is a "pointer" data type. Essentially a pointer is a unique reference to a row in a relational table. The ability to store these row IDs inside a relational table extends the traditional relational model and enhances the ability of an object-relational database to establish relationships between tables. The new abilities of pointer data types include:

Referencing "sets" of related rows in other tables

It is now possible to violate first normal form and have a cell in a table that contains a pointer to repeating table values. For example, an employee table could contain a pointer called job_history_set, which, in turn contains pointers to all of the relevant rows in a job_history table. This technique also allows for aggregate objects to be prebuilt, such that all of the specific rows that comprise the aggregate table could be preassembled.

Allow "pointers" to non-database objects in a flat file

For example, a table cell could contain a pointer to a flat file that contains a non-database object such as a picture in GIF or JPEG format.

The ability to establish one-to-many and many-to-many data relationships without relational foreign keys

This would alleviate the need for relational JOIN operations, since table columns could contain references to rows in other tables. By de-referencing these pointers, rows from other tables could be retrieved without ever using the time consuming SQL JOIN operator.

Now that we have a high-level understanding of these Oracle8 features, let's take a closer look at how they are implemented.

The Downside of Object Technology

There are several major misconceptions which must be addressed when considering the use of an object-oriented method:

1. **Object-oriented development is not a panacea.**   Object-oriented development is best suited for dynamic, interactive environments, as evidenced by its widespread acceptance in CAD/CAM and engineering design systems. Wide-scale object-oriented corporate systems are still unproved, and many bread-and-butter information systems applications (i.e., payroll, accounting) may not benefit from the object-oriented approach.

2. **Object-oriented development is not a technology.**   Although many advocates are religious in their fervor for object-oriented systems, remember that all the "HOOPLA" is directed at the object-oriented approach to problem solving, and not to any specific technology.

3. **Object-oriented development is not yet completely accepted by major vendors.** Object-oriented development has gained some market respectability, and vendors have gone from catering to a "lunatic fringe" to a respected market. Still, there are major reservations as to whether Object-oriented development will become a major force, or fade into history, as in the 1980s when Decision Support Systems made great promises, only to fade into obscurity.

4. **Cannot find qualified programmers and database administrators.** When one investigates the general acceptance of object-oriented systems in the commercial marketplace, you generally find that most managers would like to see an object technology approach, but they do not have the time to train their staff in object-oriented methods. Other will say that the object-oriented method is only for graphical workstation systems, and that there is no pressing need for object-oriented system within mainstream business systems.

   Although commercial object-oriented programming languages have been on the market for several years, systems written with object-oriented languages comprise less than 1% of systems today.

5. **Lack of standards.** Once a major vendor begins conforming to a standard, it can become impossible to retrofit their standard to conform to another standard. When the American Standards Committee came out with a standard character set for computers (ASCII), IBM disregarded the standard and proceeded with their own character set, called the Extended Binary Character Data Interchange Code (EBCDIC). Even thirty years later, there has still been no resolution between ASCII and EBCDIC, and data transfers between ASCII and EBCDIC machines continue to present problems. For example, the EBCDIC character set has no characters for "[" and "]", and ASCII has no character for the "cent" sign.

Summary

Once all of the confusing acronyms and jargon have been stripped away, the object technology approach is nothing more than a method, an approach to systems design which can be implemented without any changes to existing software technology. Now that we have provided a historical overview of database objects, we can move on to take an in-depth look at the many issues surrounding the evolving database model, and see how object technology will become an integral part of the database engines.

2

The History of Database Management and Object Management

In order to appreciate the database object model, it is important to understand all of the phases of database evolution and to examine the salient features of each successive model. In this chapter we will review the evolution of database management from pre-database systems to today's object-technology databases with a focus on how these data structures apply to database object technology. We will also examine the hybrid database architectures including the object/relational hybrid and explain why this approach has become popular for certain applications. The aim of this chapter is to demonstrate how each new database architecture added features and to introduce the concepts behind each of the database architectures. This historical perspective will help gain insight into the present state of database objects.

Pre-Database Information Storage

It is important to remember that the information organizing process precedes computers by thousand of years. The earliest known database was discovered in the 1980s in Mesopotamia, where a complete inventory management was discovered on thousands of cuneiform clay tablets. These primitive databases served the needs of their designers, illustrating that the basic data constructs of uniform storage and access methods do not necessarily require a computer. Even in the 1990s, many individuals find that a desktop rolodex file outperforms electronic files both in speed of retrieval and organization.

Flat File Processing

With the introduction of computers to the commercial public, organizations began to realize the potential of the database storage. The early computers were very large and cumbersome to maintain, but they were perfect for performing repetitive tasks such as payroll calculations, and organizations soon began to see that high-volume, repetitive data tasks such as payroll were ideal applications for these computers.

Before commercial databases were introduced, many "database" systems were really nothing more than a loosely coupled collection of flat files. These were called "flat files" because they were not linked to other files, and it was impossible to "associate" data items and establish relationships.

Flat files were physical, sequential files that were generally stored fixed-length records in a linear fashion, such that it was necessary to read the file from front-to-back to retrieve a record. Of course, indexes could be created to speed data retrieval, but these flat-file systems were still bound by their linear nature.

To add a record to a flat file, the entire file had to be read, the new record inserted in its proper sequence, and the entire file rewritten. In essence, a flat file is updated by merging the existing master file with a new data file and the outcome was a new master file. (Figure 2.1) The result of merging the old master file with a daily transaction file created an audit trail, such that the old master tapes reflected the content of the file at any given time.

To find a record in a sequential file, the system starts at the beginning of the file, and reads the file, one record at a time, until it finds the desired record. Again, the point is that it is impossible to update any record in a physical-sequential file without rewriting the entire file. Magnetic tape is an ideal media for flat files since both the file and the media are linear, and tape

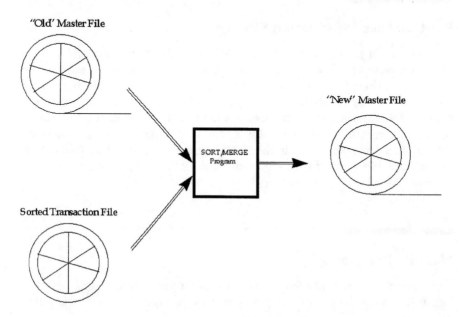

Figure 2.1   Physical-sequential file updating.

storage costs 10,000 times less than disk storage. It is interesting to note that in 1998, more data is stored in physical–sequential formats than in all other file formats. Companies are still using flat-file architecture because of systems that contain large amounts of unchanging, infrequently used data. Magnetic tapes, which are 10,000 times cheaper than disk, are still the most economical way to store large volumes of data.

So why talk about this antiquated method of file storage? It turns out that the Common Object Request Broker Architecture (CORBA) specifications allows for physical sequential files to be passed as database objects in a distributed environment. Hence, we should not discount flat files simply because of their simplicity.

Physical-sequential files are said to be non-keyed files because they must always be retrieved in the same order. The terms "QSAM" (pronounced que-sam) and "BSAM" (pronounced bee-sam) were often used to describe physical sequential files in an IBM mainframe environment. BSAM stands for the Basic Sequential Access Method, and QSAM stands for the Queued Sequential Access Method (QSAM).

Basic Direct Access Method (BDAM)

As more data was being stored on disks, organizations struggled to circumvent the linear nature of flat-file organization. When storing records on disk, each block can be identified by a unique disk address. When we know the address of a record in disk, it can very quickly be retrieved for viewing. But how do we gather the disk address for records?

Unlike physical-sequential files, the BDAM (pronounced bee-damn) method uses a hashing algorithm to determine the target address when a record is stored on disk. This accepts a symbolic key, which is usually a part of the record that is being stored, and uses the value of the symbolic key as input into a formula that will generate a unique disk address. The BDAM hashing algorithm will compute the target location of the record on the disk and then tell the access method to get the record at that location. Since we can go directly to the record, BDAM provides much faster access and retrieval of records. A direct access file is sometimes called a "keyed" file because the key is used to generate the disk address (Figure 2.2).

Just as your home address uniquely identifies where you live, a disk address identifies where a record lives on the device. A disk address includes the disk number, cylinder address, the track, and the block address. To find a record in a direct access file, the program must have a key provided so that it can determine the record address and then retrieve the desired record, regardless of all the other records in the file. The BDAM storage method was the first time that there had been a separation between the physical access

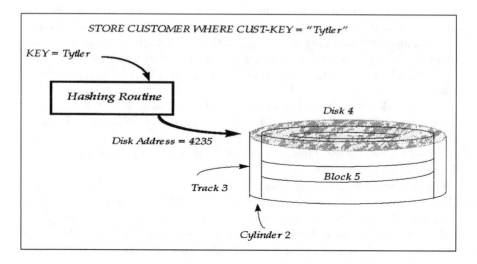

Figure 2.2   Hashed file storage.

methods and the logical access methods. That is, the record could be retrieved simply by providing the key field, and the user need not be concerned with where the record was physically located on the disk.

Unfortunately, the range of addresses which were generated by the hashing algorithm required careful management. A hashing algorithm has to be repeatable, so that the same key always returns the same disk address. BDAM has to be able to store a record with the hashing algorithm and be able to retrieve the record using the same algorithm. Also, when using a symbolic key to generate addresses, duplicate keys must be avoided. The duplication of symbolic keys (and the resulting duplicated disk addresses) leads to "collisions" whereby the hashing algorithm cannot differentiate between two records. Hence, it is critical that a unique key be created for each and every record in the file. If a single field cannot uniquely identify the records, then a combination of fields, or portions of fields can be used.

Today, we see many areas where BDAM storage is used. Consider the codes found on magazine subscription labels. These are called "concatenated" keys, and they contain pieces of fields in the base record, such as the first four letters of the subscribers last name, and a portion of the zip code. Fortunately, there are many ways to generate unique keys.

We must remember that BDAM storage does not come without a cost. Compared to physical sequential files, BDAM structures consume a large amount of disk storage. As we can infer from the storage method, BDAM files do not make efficient use of disk storage since records are randomly distributed across the disk device. Consequently, it is common to see hashed files with more unused spaces than occupied space see Figure 2.3. Unfortunately, the free space between records in a BDAM file cannot be used for any other

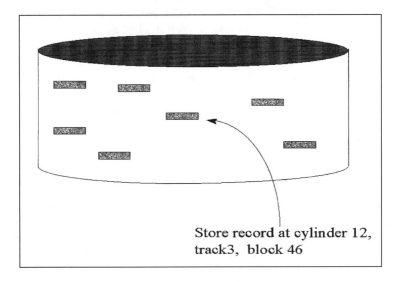

Figure 2.3 The random distribution of BDAM records.

purpose, since a future record may target to any possible address on the disk. Hence, BDAM required an exclusive disk partition.

In most cases, a BDAM file is considered "logically" full if more than 70% of the disk storage space contains data records. Maintenance of BDAM files generally requires export import operations. For example, when a BDAM files reaches 70% of capacity, the files are retrieved onto a physical-sequential file, the BDAM partition is dropped and re-allocated into a large space. To allow for the hash to generate a wider range of disk addresses, the upper and lower address limits for BDAM can be controlled, so that records can be stored on a single cylinder, a group of cylinders, or a group of disk devices.

Despite the problems of space usage and unique keys, BDAM hash files remain one of the fastest ways to store and retrieve information. Most computers can convert a symbolic key into a disk storage address in microseconds, and can store or retrieve a record in milliseconds. Although hashing is a very old technique, it is still an extremely powerful method. Even today, many C++ programmers use hashing to store and retrieve records from within their object-oriented applications.

The Indexed Sequential Access Method

While the BDAM method provides for lightning fast storage and retrieval of information, the high cost of disk storage made BDAM a very expensive proposition. However, the use of flat files with indexes to speed data retrieval became a very popular alternative to BDAM, and soon proprietary indexing methods were introduced for use with flat files. Several popular tools included ISAM (Indexed Sequential Access Method) and VSAM (Virtual Storage Access Method).

To understand indexing, let's take an example from a book. Just as you use an index in a book to find what you want quickly, a computer index can speed the retrieval of information. In the simplest index structures, the index only contains two fields. One field is the symbolic key and the second field contains the disk address of the record that contains the key value. In most file management systems, the index file is kept as a completely separate file from the master file.

When a record is requested (based upon an index key) the program will scan the index, locate the symbolic key, and then retrieve the record from the file based upon the location that was specified in the index column. (Figure 2.4) In this fashion, a flat file can be logically reorganized to retrieve record in any desired order, regardless of the physical sequencing of the data. As new records are added to the end of the master table, the ISAM file system will automatically adjust the indexes to account for the change.

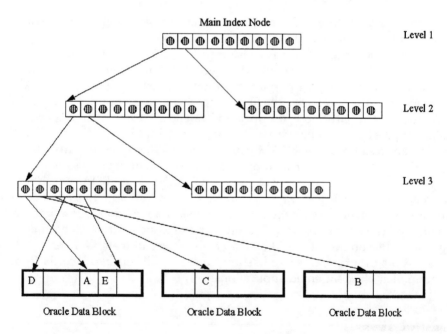

Figure 2.4   A sample index retrieval.

ISAM, like physical sequential files, stores the records back-to-back, making for very efficient use of disk space, with only the interblock gap (IBG) between records. However, unlike physical sequential format which may be stored on tape, ISAM files must be stored on disk since disk addresses are needed to create the indexes. The physical sequence of the records within

ISAM is not important since the indexes take care of the access to the records. A single ISAM file may have many dozens of indexes, each allowing the files to be retrieved in some predefined order. In some cases, the size of the indexes will exceed the size of the master file, but this is still less expensive than the disk wastage that occurs with BDAM files.

An index can be thought of as a tree, or as some call it, an "inverted" tree (Figure 2.5). The term "file inversion" is commonly used to describe the process of creating indexes, but this term is very misleading, because inversion has nothing to do with turning anything upside-down. Rather, it refers to the process of creating an index. For example, many old-timers still call creating an index on customer_number as, "inverting a file on customer_number".

Note that it is also possible to create indexes on BDAM files, permitting both fast retrieval and storage of records, as well as indexing for artificial sequencing of records are possible. BDAM record storage with indexes is still commonly used in systems that required very fast data access speeds.

Another popular file-access method was introduced by IBM, called the Virtual Storage Access Method or VSAM. VSAM combines the best features of QSAM and ISAM with additional functionality. VSAM, like its cousin ISAM, allows for physical sequential files to be indexed on multiple data items. By having multiple indexes, data can be retrieved directly in several ways and you can access data anywhere in the file using a different index.

Shortcomings of Flat Files

Needless to say, there were many problems and difficulties with flat-file database systems, especially when sharing data across applications was required. Before the invention of centralized computer resources, each department within an organization would develop their own system, usually implementing their own unique file structures and programming languages. Because of this, "islands of information" sprang-up within companies and it was very difficult for departments to share information. Duplication of data was also a major problem, since many departments within a company would often duplicate another departments data, leading to higher disk storage costs. Finally, if one department updated a redundant data item and another department did not synchronize the update, data discrepancies would result, and the values would not be uniform at each location.

But these were only a part of the problem with flat files. If a file structure ever changed, trying to identify all of the programs that needed modification was almost impossible. In addition, flat files possessed no real backup and recovery methods. Programmers had to write programs to backup a system before updates started. If a failure occurred at any time during the update run, the files were corrupted and they had to restore from the backup and rerun the update from the beginning. Another perplexing problem was that there was no standard method for accessing the data and no uniform format for the storage of data. One application might require Cobol while another used Fortran, and one program might store a number as compressed binary while another system stored the same number in a hexadecimal format.

Now that we understand the basic file storage methods, let's take a look at how they can be combined to form what is known as a database management system. Remember, a DBMS data subsystem is really nothing more than a cohesive collection of basic data structures. Despite all of the hoopla about modeling complex database objects, virtually every conceivable data structure in a state-of-the-art database system are basic data structures that have been around for decades.

The Era of Formal Database Management

Databases were first developed as a direct result of the shortcomings of flat-file systems. Prior to database management, data resided in vastly different internal formats, and data was not managed in a consistent fashion. Even more onerous, the pre-database systems were extremely difficult to communicate with other data systems. It is important to remember that a database management systems provides far more than just a uniform repository for information. All database management systems provide the following features:

1. Recovery of incomplete transactions (rollback).
2. A mechanism for recovering transactions after disk failure (roll forward).
3. Internal tools for the management of relationships between data.
4. Locking and concurrency tools for simultaneous multiple user access.
5. A common access language that can be embedded in procedural code.

The database management systems of the 1990s also provide:

1. Internal support for maintaining business rules (referential integrity).
2. Read consistency for long-running queries.
3. Support for distributed updates (two-phase commit).
4. Support for modeling complex objects.
5. Attaching behaviors to data (methods).

The early Database Managers access methods were based on BDAM or VSAM and indexes were often created to speed-up data access. In the late 1950s, IBM developed a prototype computer database to demonstrate that data could be stored, retrieved, and updated in a structured format. This database became known as the Information Management System, or IMS. IMS was a revolutionary idea since it allows data access by numerous programs in different languages and was designed to support the multiuser needs of larger organizations. Even more important, the creation of IMS codified the industries belief that data was important, and needed to be managed and controlled in a consistent fashion.

The Hierarchical Database Model

As we noted, the major difference between flat-file systems and a DBMS is the ability to store both data as well as the relationships between the data. The hierarchical database model was first introduced as IMS (Information Management System), which was released in 1960. The hierarchical database model used pointers to logically link related data items, and it does this with the use of child" and "twin" pointers. In 1998, IMS still enjoys a large following among users with large databases and high-volume transaction requirements. A Hierarchical database is very well suited to modeling relationships that are naturally hierarchical. For example, within an organization, we see that each executive has many managers, each manager has many supervisors, and each supervisor has many workers. Basically, a hierarchy is a method of organizing data into descending one-to-many relationships, with each level in the hierarchy having a higher precedence than those below it.

A hierarchy is just an arrangement of structures called nodes, and the nodes are connected by lines or "branches." You can think of these lines or branches as a connection to the next level of more specific information. The highest node is called the root node, and queries must pass through this node on their way down the hierarchy. In our example (Figure 2.5), UNIVERSITY is the root node. Every node, except the root node, is connected upward to only one "parent" node. Nodes have a parent-child relationship, and a parent node is directly above the child node. We also see that the node called COLLEGE OF ENGINEERING is a parent of ELECTRICAL ENGINEERING. Since a child node is always one level directly below its parent node, the ELECTRICAL ENGINEERING node is a child of the COLLEGE OF ENGINEERING node. Note that a parent node can have more than one child node, but a child may only have one parent.

When we talk about a hierarchical database, the nodes that we talked about become "segment types." A segment type is simply a user-defined category of data, and each segment contains fields. Each segment has a key field, and the key field is used to retrieve the data from the segment. There can be one or more fields in a segment, and most segments also contain multiple search fields.

Expanding on Figure 2.5, let's add some data fields to our UNIVERSITY segment. Let's begin by describing the data for each UNIVERSITY. UNIVERSITY information might include the UNIVERSITY name, the mailing address, and phone number.

IMS is well-suited for modeling systems in which the entities (segments) are composed of descending one-to-many relationships. Relationships are established with "child" and "twin" pointers, and these pointers are embedded into the prefix of every record in the database.

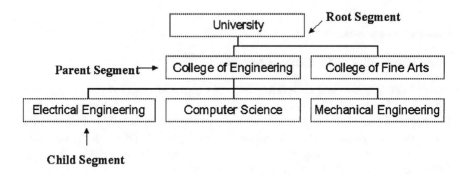

Figure 2.5 A sample hierarchical chart.

Referring to Figure 2.5, we see six segments:

1. UNIVERSITY
2. COLLEGE OF ENGINEERING
3. COLLEGE OF FINE ARTS
4. ELECTRICAL ENGINEERING
5. COMPUTER SCIENCE
6. MECHANICAL ENGINEERING

We also have four hierarchical paths:

1. UNIVERSITY, COLLEGE OF ENGINEERING, ELECTRICAL ENGINEERING
2. UNIVERSITY, COLLEGE OF ENGINEERING, COMPUTER SCIENCE
3. UNIVERSITY, COLLEGE OF ENGINEERING, MECHANICAL ENGINEERING
4. UNIVERSITY, COLLEGE OF FINE ARTS

A hierarchical path defines the access method, and the path is like an imaginary line that begins at the root segment and passes through segment types until it reaches the segment type at the bottom of the inverted tree. One advantage to a hierarchical database is that if you only wanted information on COLLEGES, the program would only have to know the format and access the store segment. You would not have to know that any of the other five segments even exist, what their fields are, or what relationship exists between the segments.

Hierarchical databases have rigid rules in relationships and data access. For example, all segments have to be accessed through the parent segment. The exception to this is, of course, the root segment because it has no parent.

The IMS database has concurrent control, and a full backup and recovery mechanism. The backup and recovery protects the system from a failure of IMS itself, an application program, a database failure, and a operating system failure. The recovery mechanism for application programs stores "before" and "after" images of each record which was changed, and these images could be used to "roll-back" the database if a transaction failed to complete. If there was a disk failure the images could be "rolled-forward." IMS was used with the CICS teleprocessing monitor to develop the first on-line database systems for the mainframe.

Three main advantages of hierarchical databases are: (1) a large base with a proven technology that has been around for decades, (2) the ease of using a hierarchy or tree structure, and (3) the speed of the system (exceeding 2000 transactions per second). Some disadvantages of hierarchical databases are because of rigid rules in relationships, insertion and deletion can become very complex, access to a child segment can only be done through the parent segment (start at the root segment). While IMS is very good at modeling hierarchical data relationships, complex data relationships such as many-to-many and recursive many-to-many, like BOM (bill-of-material) relationships had to be implemented in a very clumsy fashion, by using "phantom" records. The IMS database also suffered from its complexity. To become proficient in IMS you need months of training and experience. As a result, IMS development remains very slow and cumbersome.

Just like hierarchical databases use pointers to logically relate records together, database object implementations also use pointers to link objects. Generally, database objects are linked using their object IDs just like hierarchical records are linked with pointers. It is also common to see naturally occurring hierarchies to be represented with permutations of the child–twin pointer methods.

The CODASYL Network Model

During the 1960s, several major DBMS products were created using the CODASYL Network Database Management System (DBMS) specifications developed by the Conference on Data Systems Languages (CODASYL). Also involved were two subgroups of CODASYL: the Database Task Group (DBTG) and the Data Description Language Committee (DDLC).

CODASYL and its subgroups are an organization of volunteer representatives of computer manufacturers and users. While CODASYL began in 1959, the first set of DBMS specifications were not produced until 1969. This set of specifications was revised, and the first real CODASYL DBTG specifications were issued in 1971.

Basically, all database management systems share some features with CODASYL DBTG specifications. From the early CODASYL DBTG specs, the data model was called a "Network" data model, and the model that CODASYL DBTG developed became the basis for new database systems like IDMS from Cullinet in 1970.

The Data Base Task Group (DBTG) CODASYL Specifications included Schema definition, Device Media Control Language (DMCL) definition, Data Manipulation Language (DML) definition. It also included the concept of a database "area" which referred to the physical structure of the data files. The Logical Structure of the database was defined by a Data Definition Language (DDL), and a user view of the data was defined by a subschema.

The Data Manipulation Language (DML) commands were used to navigate through the linked-list structures that comprised the database, much the same as object-oriented databases are navigated in C++. The CODASYL DML verbs included FIND, GET, STORE, MODIFY, and DELETE.

The Data Base Administrator (DBA) functions in a CODASYL database included: data structure or schema, data integrity, security, and authorization. Also a Data Base Manager (DBM) function was defined which included: operation, backup/recovery, performance, statistics, auditing.

The CODASYL model used two data storage methods, BDAM and linked-list data structure, and BDAM used a hashing algorithm to store and retrieve records.

Because of the many choices that can be made in the design of a Network database, it is important to review the design with as many people as possible. Charles Bachman developed a "diagram" that represented the data structures as required by CODASYL. This diagram method became known as the Bachman diagram (Figure 2.6.)

The Bachman diagram describes the physical constructs of all record types in the database. The rectangles of the Bachman diagram are subdivided into four rows. The top row of the box contains the record name. Row two contains the numeric identification ID number (each record is given a number which is associated with the record name), the length mode which is fixed or variable, the length of the records, and the location mode (CALC, or VIA). Row three contains for CALC, the field serving as the CALC key, and for VIA SET, the set name. Row four contains the area designated. The set type is

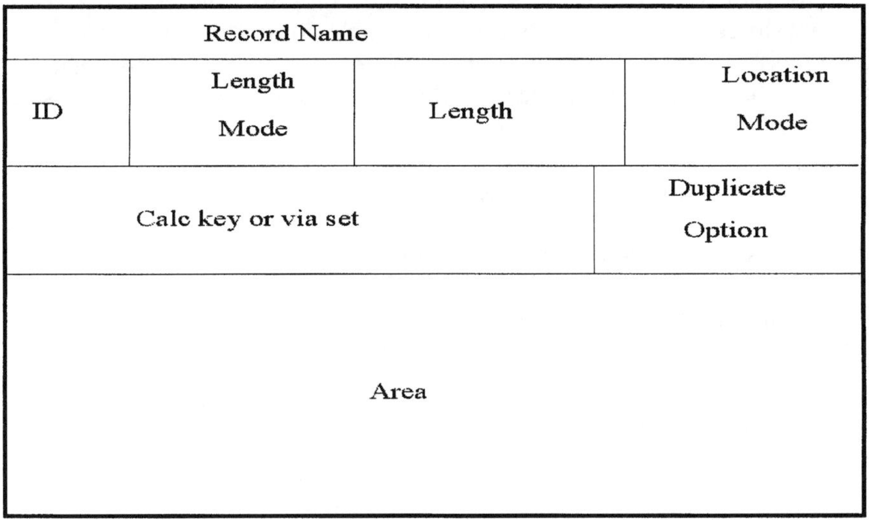

Record Name			
ID	Length Mode	Length	Location Mode
Calc key or via set			Duplicate Option
Area			

Figure 2.6   Bachman diagram layout.

shown by a Bachman arrow pointing from the owner record type to the member record type. See Figure 2.7. Set name is the owner name hyphen member name. Pointers are Next, Prior and Owner; the membership option is used for insertion and retention (MA, OA, MM, OM); the set order is (First, Last, Next, Prior, or Sorted); and the mode is (Chain or Index).

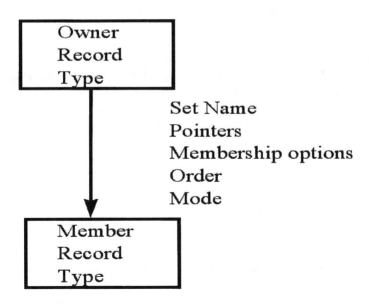

Figure 2.7   Bachman set type.

Some database records are stored using hashing techniques, and records that are stored "CALC" use a symbolic key to determine the physical location of the record. In a CODASYL database records are allowed to be clustered. Records that have "VIA" indicate that they are stored on the same physical data blocks as their owner records. Data relationships are established by using "sets", which link the relationships together. For example, the ORDER-LINE records are physically clustered near their ITEM records. This is indicated in the Bachman diagram (Figure 2.8) where the ORDER-LINE box shows VIA as the location mode, and the ORDER-ITEM relationship as the cluster set. The Bachman diagram is still used today. It is a very useful graphical picture of the database schema.

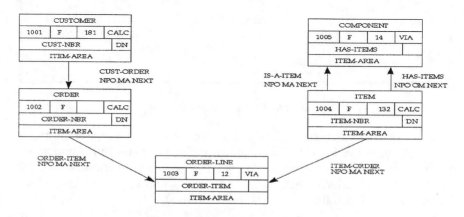

Figure 2.8 Bachman diagram example.

The CODASYL model combined two data storage methods to create an engine which was capable of producing hundreds of transactions per second. The CODASYL model uses the basic direct access method (BDAM) which uses a hashing algorithm (sometimes called a CALC algorithm) to quickly store and retrieve records. CODASYL also employs linked-list data structures, that create embedded pointers in the prefix of each occurrence of a record. These pointers, called NEXT, PRIOR, and OWNER, are used to establish relationships between data items and are referenced in the Data Manipulation Language (DML). For example, the DML command OBTAIN NEXT ORDER WITHIN CUSTOMER-ORDER, would direct the network database to look in the prefix of the current ORDER record, and find the NEXT pointer for the CUSTOMER-ORDER set. The database will then access the record who's address is found at this location.

Two advantages to the CODASYL approach were the fast performance and the ability to represent complex data relationships. The following example shows how BDAM is invoked for the OBTAIN CALC CUSTOMER statement, and linked lists are used in the statement OBTAIN NEXT CUSTOMER WITHIN CUSTOMER-ORDER.

This example shows how to navigate a one-to-many relationship, (i.e. to get all of the orders for a customer), a CODASYL programmer would enter:

```
MOVE 'MS' to CUST-DESC.
OBTAIN CALC CUSTOMER.
PERFORM ORDER-LOOP UNTIL END-OF-SET.
ORDER-LOOP.
    OBTAIN NEXT ORDER WITHIN CUSTOMER-ORDER.
    MOVE ORDER-NBR TO OUT-REC.
    WRITE OUT-REC.
```

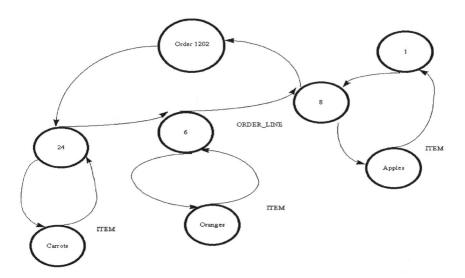

Figure 2.9   Set occurrence diagram.

The CODASYL set occurrence diagram (Figure 2.9), used as a visual tool has been resurrected for use in object-oriented databases. The relationships between objects become readily apparent, and a programmer can easily envision the navigation paths. For example, in Figure 2.9, you can easily see that order 1202 is for 24 carrots, 6 oranges, and 8 apples. Now look at the "item" side of the diagram, and you can easily see which orders include apples. When you are working with systems that physically link objects, the set occurrence diagram is an extremely useful visual tool.

The design of the CODASYL network model was very complex, and consequently very difficult to use. Network databases, very much like hierarchical databases, are very difficult to navigate. The Data Manipulation Language (DML), designed for complex navigation, was a skill that required months of training.

Implementing structural changes was extremely difficult with network databases since data relationships are "hard-linked" with embedded pointers. Adding an index or a new relationship requires special utility programs that will "sweep" each and every affected record in the database. As records are located, the prefix is restructured to accommodate the new pointers. Object-oriented databases will encounter this same problem if a class hierarchy needs to be modified.

Even with these shortcomings, CODASYL databases were still far superior to any other technology of the day, and many corporations began to implement their mission-critical systems on IDMS platforms. However, as soon as relational databases solved their speed problems and became stable enough to support mission-critical systems, the awkward and inflexible CODASYL systems were abandoned.

CODASYL and the Object Database Management Group (ODMG)

Even though the CODASYL model is more than 25 years old, it is fascinating to note that there is a remarkable similarity between the CODASYL model and the internal models of today's state-of-the-art object databases.

Just as the CODASYL model required a CALC to uniquely identify a record, object databases require an "Object ID" or OID (pronounced oy-id) to identify an object.

Unfortunately, relational database models cannot address the high overhead and potential problems involved in generating OBJECT IDs. Some theoreticians have proposed a data model which allow a single field to contain multiple values, or even another table, such as Dr. Won Kim's UniSQL database. In a procedural language such as C++, the problem of recursion is addressed very elegantly with pointers to structures.

The ODMG standard for object-oriented databases requires unique object IDs to identify each object, and they have deliberately not addressed the ability to access a row, based on the data contents of the row.

Many researchers have noted remarkable similarities between the CODASYL Network Model (NWM), and the requirements for object-oriented databases. The CODASYL model supports the declaration of abstract "sets" to relate classes together, and CODASYL also supports the notion of "currency," whereby a record may be accessed without any reference to its data attributes. CODASYL databases provide currency tables that allow the programmer to "remember" the most recently accessed record of each type, and the most recently accessed record within a set.

Object database researchers, Schek and Scholl, state, "This shows that some of the essential features of the object model can be found in the CODASYL; CODASYL records are instances of abstract types manipulated by a limited set of functions (called FINDs), mostly for navigational access. CONNECT and DISCONNECT are used to add or remove objects to or from relationships. Finally, GET retrieves data about the objects into a predefined communications area."

Of all of the existing database models, the CODASYL network model most closely matches the requirements for object-oriented databases, and with some refinement (such as the support of "cyclic" data relationships), the CODASYL model may re-emerge in a new form, as the standard data model for object-oriented modeling.

Some vendors are already using the CODASYL model as the architecture for object-oriented databases. For example, the C-Data Manager from Database Technologies, is an object-oriented database and programming environment which is based on the CODASYL Network Data Model, and uses ISAM file structures to index its data records.

The Relational Database Model

In 1970, Dr. Edgar (Ted) Codd of IBM developed a Relational Model of Data. In the model, data would be stored in simple linear files, these simple linear files are called "relations" or "tables". One of the best improvements of the relational model over its predecessors was its simplicity. Rather than having to know dozens of DML commands, the relational model introduced a declarative language called Structured Query Language (SQL) to simplify data access and manipulation.

Codd chose to call his language "Structured Query Language" because it is not structured, it is not only for queries (SQL can update), and it is not a language (it is embedded in languages).

The tables are two-dimensional arrays of "rows" and "columns." Rows are sometimes called "tuples" (rhymes with "couples") and columns are sometimes called "attributes." A "record" is a row of a table, and a "field" is a column, in a row of a table. A table will always have a field or several fields that make a "primary key" for a table. In a relational database, the tables are independent, unlike hierarchical and network models that are pointer connected. Tables basically correspond to segment types in hierarchical and record types in the network models. Relational tables can contain only one type of record, and each record has a fixed number of fields that are all explicitly named. There is no predetermined sequence of records in a table and duplicate records are not allowed in a table, also in a table, fields are distinct and repeating groups are not allowed (Figure 2.10).

A primary key uniquely identifies a row in a table, the key can be made up of one or more fields. A foreign key allows you to join two or more tables together by using a key field in one table with a non key field in another table.

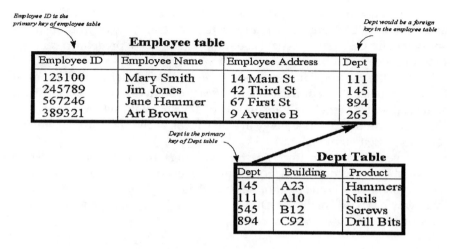

Figure 2.10   A sample relational chart.

Relational databases made the following improvements over hierarchical and network databases:

1. **Simplicity** — The concept of tables with rows and columns is extremely simple and easy to understand. End users have a simple data model. Complex network diagrams used with the hierarchical and network databases are not used with a relational database.

2. **Data independence** — Data independence is the ability to modify data structures (in this case, tables) without affecting existing programs. Much of this is because tables are not hard-linked to one another. Columns can be added to tables, tables can be added to the database, and new data relationships can be added with little or no restructuring of the tables. A relational database provides a much higher degree of data independence than do hierarchical and network databases.

3. **Declarative data access** — The SQL user specifies what data they want, then the embedded SQL (Structural Query Language), a procedural language determines how to get the data. In relational database access, the user tells the system the conditions for the retrieval of data. The system then gets the data that meets the selection conditions in the SQL statements. The database navigation is hidden from the end user or programmer, unlike a CODA-SYL DML language, where the programmer had to know the details of the access path.

Dr. Codd also introduced with the relational database, the concept of Structured Query Language (SQL), also known as "sequel." SQL was much more than a query language. SQL is really a data sub-language that supports end-users, programmers, database administrators, and security administrators.

There are two ways to think of SQL. The first says that SQL can be thought of as having three categories of function: Define, Manipulate, and Authorize. Define is the DDL that does create, drop, and alter functions. Manipulate is the DML that does select, insert, update, and delete functions. Authorize is the control that does grant and revoke functions. Within the DML functions, the other school teaches that SQL has three DML functions: Select, Project, and Join. A select reduced the length of a table by filtering out unwanted rows, a project shrinks the width of the table by filtering out unwanted columns, and a join is used to relate two or more independent tables that share a common column.

The most important point about SQL is that it allowed programmers and end users a simple, easy way to add, change, and extract data from a relational database. Any two or more tables could be joined together on the fly at run time using their primary and/or foreign keys. There are no pointers or hard links from one table to another.

The Object-Oriented Database Model

While the idea of objects has been with us since the start of data processing, there has been an evolution toward what are know as object databases. The first procedural languages to couple data with behavior was the simula language, which was used in operations research tasks to simulate the behavior of entities. Objects in a data management sense was first developed by Xerox Corporation's Palo Alto Research Center in the early 1970s. In Object-Oriented databases, the focus is on objects, not functions. Object-oriented (OO) technology requires a totally new mindset, developers create models that are mapped to real world processes.

The object-oriented approach emphasizes a more natural representation of the data. In today's environment, the data models are more demanding. They need to handle audio, video, text, graphics, etc. These requirements demand a more flexible storage format than hierarchical, network, and relational databases can provide. Only object-oriented databases will be able to support this kind of demand.

Three of the fundamentals of object-oriented technology are classes, objects, and messages. A class describes a group of objects that have common relationships, behaviors, and also have similar properties. An object encompasses related data and functions into a completely self contained package. Because objects are "stamped" out from a common class definition, each instance of an object within a class inherits all of the same behaviors and data definitions. The heart of an object-oriented database is object persistence, and it is the process of storing and retrieving objects that comprises the heart of object data management.

A database object may have a different OID each time that it is loaded onto the heap (memory), and the OODBMS must manage and assign the OIDs according to the memory location after the object has been retrieved from disk..

Let's take a look at how behaviors or methods are invoked within an object database. For example, assume that we have an object of class order with an object id of 123. The object oriented call to compute the total of order 123 might look like this:

```
order.compute_order_total(123);
```

In this case, the message compute_order_total is being sent to the order class definition along with the OID that will be the target of the message. A method by the name compute_order_total will then be executed against order 123 and the desired data manipulation will take place.

In distributed systems, messaging becomes more important because the class definitions that contain the behaviors may reside on geographically remote processors. For more information on distributed message processing see Chapter 7, "Distributed Object Technology and Database Management."

Each time an object is created, a unique OID (object identifier) is added to the OODBMS (object-oriented database management system) identifier table. When an application references an object via its OID, the OODBMS converts the OID into a virtual memory address. This means that the object can be found quickly regardless of where it is stored, i.e., local memory, a remote hard disk, or on a device in a networked system. The OID is independent of the value of an object or any data contained in the object. You can change any or all of the variables in an object and the system will still access the correct object. An OID once assigned to an object by the system, lasts the lifetime of an object. An OID is much different from the concept of a key in a relational database. In a relational database, the key, is defined by one or more values of the fields of a table. The key in a relational table can be modified. In an OODBMS, the identity of an object is system generated and cannot be changed. Any two objects are different because of their OID, even if they have the same value.

Let's see how OODBMS relate to RDBMS. Object classes correspond to relational tables, object attributes correspond to columns, and instances of objects correspond to rows in a table. Objects are related to each other by the OID, this corresponds to primary and foreign keys in the relational model. For more information on this technique, see Chapter 9, "Interfacing an Object-Oriented Application with a Relational Database."

The object technology model also provides for the encapsulation of data and operations inside an object. As long as the external interfaces remain unchanged, developers can modify encapsulated data and operations in an object without affecting other objects. Encapsulation makes the data and procedures private within an object.

As you can see, OODBMS have many new terms, concepts and ways of doing things. The potential benefits of the object databases are faster development, higher quality, easier maintenance, and increased salability and adaptability. In addition the object databases claim to allow the MIS personnel to better model the real-world, resulting in better information structures and reduced costs for systems. Potential concerns with object databases are:

1. Lack of maturity
2. The need for better tools
3. The need for standards
4. The availability of qualified personnel
5. The costs of data conversion

The object-oriented approach is not only concerned with data storage, data relationships, and easy data access, but also the behavior storage. This fundamental difference will revolutionize the way that databases function. Rather than having all of the DML in hundreds of external application programs, the DML will be tightly coupled with the class definition for their associated objects, and will reside in the DBMS along with the data. This implies that business processes and data will share a common ground.

Object Persistence

Object persistence is one of the most fundamental services provided by a pure OODBMS. By persistence, we mean that an object within a language such as C++ is always available and an object's state will remain unchanged from one invocation to the next. Prior to object persistence, objects were kept in RAM memory and were destroyed upon termination of the object-oriented program.

Objects that are not permanently available are called transient objects. Depending on the application, some objects may need to change their state from transient to persistent, and the OODBMS will manage the conversion from persistent to transient. The OODBMS assigns each object an object identifier (OID), this unique identifier is used primarily to establish relationships between persistent objects. OODBMS provide the recovery services that ensure persistence objects survive any kind of system failure. The ORB(Object Request Broker) will send a request for a particular object to the OODBMS, which will use the OID to retrieve and invoke the object. There are two methods that the OODBMS uses to access persistent objects, virtual memory address pointers and hash tables. A persistent object will always be ready to be invoked, and its state can and will be preserved and survive any kind of system failure. Remember, persistent objects are stored on disk and transient objects exist in RAM memory. In an OODBMS, an object may traverse between states, having a RAM representation as well as a disk representation of the object.

The following are some of the actions that a OODBMS will perform for object persistence, the most important, of course, being the management of objects as they are retrieved from disk and assigned new OIDs in RAM memory. At the lowest level an OODBMS:

1. Assigns and allocates space in persistent storage
2. Automatically increase space when needed
3. Manages the free space in persistence storage
4. Interfaces with the I/O system with persistent storage
5. Ensures that persistent objects can be recovered
6. Manages the database buffers
7. Manages the mappings between the physical addresses and the OIDs.

Now that we have a general understanding of the role of a data persistence manager within an object-oriented language, let's take a look at the work being done by the Object Database Management Group to define standards for object persistence.

The Object Database Management Group (ODMG)

The ODMG (Object Database Management Group) will be covered in detail in Chapter 5. This is an introduction to the function and purpose of the ODMG. The ODMG is a subgroup of the OMG (Object Management Group). The OMG is a consortium of hundreds of object vendors whose purpose is setting standards for object technology. The ODMG is the standards-setting group for object database technology that is made up of a consortium of object-oriented DBMS vendors.

In 1993, the first release of the ODMG was published called ODMG-93, by members of the Object Database Management Group (ODMG). This was the result of over a year's work defining standards for OODBS (Object-Oriented Database System). The ODMG-93 standard included a common architecture and definition for an OODBMS, definitions for an object model, an object definition language (ODL), an object query language (OQL), and for bindings to

C++ and SmallTalk. ODMG-93 used the OMG object model as it's starting point and then extended it for database needs.

As a result of ODMG-93 and the standards that were created applications become more portable and the whole OODBMS (Object Oriented Database Management System) technology received a much needed uplift. The ODMG-93 model will be updated as needed and new releases will be published by the ODMG.

The Object/Relational Database Model

The object/relational database is the latest in the on-going craze of hybrid database architectures. This model has come about because of the large investment that corporate America has in relational databases and the large retraining effort that would be involved to go from relational to object-oriented databases.

OODBMS lack some of the features that all users and the information systems community have come to expect: simple and easy query capabilities like relational SQL, excellent OLTP (On-Line Transaction Processing), and an independent software industry providing utilities and application solutions. OODBMS at the present time do not have the infrastructure in place to overtake relational databases as relational did to hierarchical and network databases.

The solution for companies like Oracle, Informix, Sybase, and IBM is to extend their existing engines, transforming them into an OR (object/relational) database. These database architectures enhance the relational database by adding an object infrastructure and building relational extenders. The object infrastructure is added to the database to support numerous object features including user defined data types, rules, and functions. Relational extenders are needed to handle complex objects, and support for polymorphism and inheritance.

The Object/relational databases are gaining support because many organizations are finding that the relational database model is not robust enough to support their complex processing requirements. Rather than jumping directly into pure object-oriented technology, with its high learning curve, the object/relational approach allows developers to become familiar with the object-oriented technology at a comfortable pace. They also will not have to convert their relational or other databases to the new object-oriented data formats, thereby saving both time and money. The object-relational database is a way to bridge the gap between OODBMS and RDBMS, by allowing companies to take advantage of object-oriented technology's greater productivity and complex data types without losing their existing investment in relational applications and data.

Summary

All database management systems have failed in some ways to meet the needs of their user community. To improve on the hierarchical model, the Network model was developed in the late 1960s, and the CODASYL network model was a major improvement of the hierarchical model because to provided a more elegant way of establishing many-to-many and recursive data relationships. Network databases were more flexible, but as a result, they were also more complex. The access language for network database is called Data Manipulation Language (DML) and consists of more than 35 verbs, which can be combined in hundreds of ways. Hence, DML was unavailable to end users and highly trained programmers were required to code even the most simple database query. CODASYL worked well in transaction processing environments. The CODASYL specifications that were developed by CODASYL DBTG became a cornerstone for all databases. In fact, some of the CODASYL specifications could be used in the object-oriented database specifications that the OMG group is putting together for OODBMS.

Because of the complex nature of both hierarchical and network databases users wanted and needed a simpler design. The relational model was the simpler design that was needed, but it took 10 to 15 years for computer technology to catch up. The relational model can be thought of as a collection of two dimensional arrays called tables that have rows and columns. It has a very simple and easy to use language called SQL, making ad hoc queries frequent and easy. Today, the relational model is the most widely accepted and popular database model. Even with all of the improvements that the relational model has over hierarchical and network models, and the fact that technology has, and is changing, we now have and need to store audio, video, text, graphics, etc. Users want more.

The distinguishing characteristic of the object-oriented database is its ability to store data behavior, but how does the behavior of the data get incorporated into the database? At first glance, this may seem to be a process for moving application code from a program into a database. While it is true that an object-oriented database stores "behaviors," these databases must also have the ability to manage many different objects, each with different data items.

Now that we have reviewed the basic data structures that make up a commercial database management system, we can move on to take a closer look at object-oriented systems analysis. By understanding the internals of database management and the constructs of object-oriented analysis, we can develop a firm understanding of database objects and their use in the real world.

3

Database Object Analysis and Design

The object technology approach to problem solving has several important differences from traditional data processing systems. The first and most important is the absolute necessity of thorough analysis before any coding begins. The rigid structures of object-oriented class hierarchies can make ad-hoc systems development very dangerous. For example, some of the fourth-generation languages are designed to allow the developer to create their system in an ad-hoc fashion, building screens and database tables without any formal forethought. If a data item has been forgotten, the change can be easily added to the schema with the ALTER TABLE statement. In object-oriented databases, once objects have been instantiated, changes to data structures would require time-consuming restructuring of all of the affected objects. In this scenario, each persistent object on disk must be accessed, restructured, and rewrittem to disk. Needless to say, this is a very time-consuming operation requiring significant downtime for the system.

A properly designed class hierarchy will have very low maintenance, however, it is not easily modified in an object-oriented environment, especially after persistent objects have been created. Great care must be taken to properly identify the classes, and the relationships between the classes, and all one-to-many, many-to-many, and IS-A relationships must be properly identified. Most object technology systems do not lend themselves to class modification after coding has begun, and caution must be taken to ensure that the initial design of the class hierarchy is correct.

Object-Oriented vs. Traditional Analysis

In software development, there are three main parts: analysis, design, and programming. Analysis deals with understanding the user's requirements and how these requirements can be met using the appropriate computer technology.

In many cases, systems analysis is often overlooked or done too quickly. As a result, many information systems never reach their real potential and suffer from a variety of ailments that could have been avoided with more careful analysis. Maintenance on these systems is always high, and the budget for these systems is always going through the roof because the infrastructure for the system was not properly described. It seems that many companies want results quickly and the first thing they skimp on is the effort required to perform a complete analysis and design. Many times what happens is that a system is developed in a vacuum, instead of taking the time to understand how the system will interface with other systems and what will be needed to establish proper interfaces. In almost all cases, this approach leads to high maintenance costs and slower system development time.

Many companies have found that while they could get away with a poor analysis and design, proper system analysis and design are an absolute necessity for object databases (Figure 3.1).

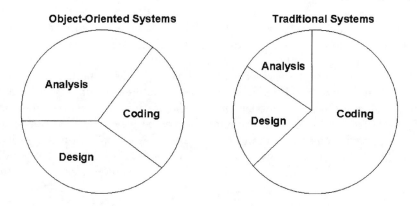

Object-Oriented Systems require more Analysis & Design effort than traditional systems

Figure 3.1   The resources used in systems development methods.

As an example, think about all of the thousands of hours of work that is required to modify systems to keep them running after the year 2000. If the original developers had been aware that these system would still be used in the late 1990s, much of the conversion headache would not have been necessary. In the 1970s when disk storage was very expensive, many companies used a two-digit year instead of a four-digit year. As a result they are now spending billions of dollars to change legacy systems whose lifespan might only be a few years after the year 2000.

As we know, there are three major activities in software development: analysis, design, and programming. (Figure 3.2) Traditional systems use the approach that when a change is needed, they modify only that which is

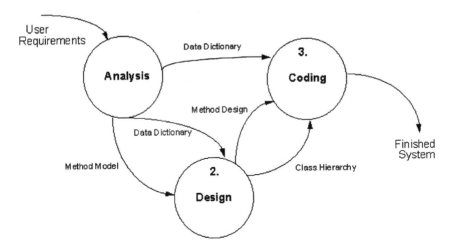

Figure 3.2   A high-level overview of systems development.

necessary. Object-oriented development uses a different approach — it requires a well-defined plan before any systems construction can be undertaken. Regardless of whether you use the traditional approach or the object-oriented approach, the gains from doing a "quality analysis" are monumental. If developers resist the temptation to start coding and spend more time thinking about the problem prior to attempting to solve the problem, many systems would be in a far better state at present. In general, an extensive systems analysis can lead to the following benefits:

- Customers get better systems at less cost.
- Projects are done on time.
- Systems organizations and companies becomes more competitive.
- Maintenance for the system is lower.
- Changes can be made to systems faster and with less cost.

One of the basic distinctions between traditional systems and object-oriented systems is the initiator for the processes. Object-oriented systems are event-driven, and unlike traditional systems where a process is triggered by the change to a data item. But how does an analyst shift from thinking about systems in the traditional way to thinking about systems as a collection of interacting objects? To understand the answer, let's take a look at object behavior analysis—a new method that:

1. Identifies a hierarchy of behaviors for the entire system.
2. Identifies the "primitive" behaviors and create a behavior hierarchy.

3. Identifies all objects which exhibit the behaviors and creates a class hierarchy.
4. Associates each primitive behavior with each object class.

The first step is to be able to identify the objects. When isolating the physical objects within the structured analysis document, it is tempting to focus on the nouns within the diagram, and assume that all "things," which represent physical objects should be modeled as objects. While this is true, this approach often ignores the intangible objects which have a tremendous bearing on the system.

The best approach to understanding a system in object-oriented terms is to change the focus from data flows to object behaviors. Behaviors are events which are generally associated with verbs, such as "Create Order Form," or "Print Service Request." To properly identify all of the behaviors within a system, it is necessary to take a very top-down approach to system behavior. At a highest level, the overall system can be said to have a behavior, although it is often quite difficult to give the system a meaningful behavior name. Often, entire systems can be labeled with names like "Process Inventory" or "Manage Personnel Records", but it is critical to the development of the object-oriented system to clearly identify each component of the system within a behavioral context.

Now that we understand the basic approach and benefits of object-oriented analysis and design, let's move on to discuss some of the more popular approaches to object database development.

Traditional Systems Analysis

There are three commonly accepted traditional methods for systems analysis: (1) the Gane & Sarson method, (2) the Yourdon method, and (3) the DeMarco systems analysis method. All three of these models share a common goal: before any physical construction of the system begins, the new system must be completely analyzed to determine the "functional primitive" processes and the data flows between the processes. This logical specification is used as the input to the systems design. But how does the systems analysis change when an object-oriented database system is being developed?

It is very important to remember that the purpose of systems analysis is to logically identify the processes, the data moving between the processes, and to describe the processing rules and data items. Only after these are defined can design begin, regardless of the physical implementation of the system. While the design strategy for an object-oriented system may be very different from other systems, object-oriented analysis should begin with the creation of a structured specification.

A structured specification is a document which describes all of the data, data storage, external entities, and processes for the system. This document is then used in the design phase for the creation of the behaviors, entity/relation model, and class hierarchy. The structured specification of a traditional systems analysis consists of the following deliverables:

1. **Data-flow diagrams** — A set of top-down diagrams depicting all of the processes within the system, the data flows between the processes, and the data stores. The data flow diagrams (DFDs) begin at a very general level and become progressively more detailed. The lowest level of processing is called the "functional primitive" level, and this primitive level has been traditionally used as the starting point for systems design.

   As shown in the DFD from Figure 3.2, there are four symbols that are used to represent entities. The first is a rectangle which represents external entities such as a vendor, another system, a customer, and so on. These external entities are called "sources" if they provide data to the DFD and "sinks" if the receive data from the DFD. The circle symbol represents a process which shows how data flows are changed. The third symbol is the arrow, which represents a data flow, and the direction of the data flow is indicated by the arrowhead. Finally we see the double line which represents a data store, which will eventually become the databases, the core of our object system.

2. **Data dictionary** — The data dictionary contains a description of all of the logical data items, including all data flows, data types, data structures and data stores (Files) that appear on the DFD.

3. **Process logic specifications (minispecs)** — A minispec is a description of all of the functional primitive processes that appear on the DFD. A process is defined as an operation which modifies a data flow. The tools used to describe processes include pseudo-code, procedure flowcharts, decision trees, and decision tables.

We should now have an general understanding of the fundamental concepts of a traditional systems analysis, and we are now ready to take a look at how analysis for object-oriented systems differs from traditional analysis.

Object Analysis and Functional Specifications

In order to properly describe the environment of an object-oriented system, the designer needs to be able to develop a conceptual framework. Object-oriented systems view the world at a much higher level than traditional systems, and unlike traditional analysis, it is no longer necessary to de-partition systems down to the data element level. Object-oriented databases view the system components as physical "objects," i.e., order forms, invoices, rather than abstract data definitions. Figure 3.3 shows an order-form object that contains the Customer, Order, and Item list objects that participate in the order form.

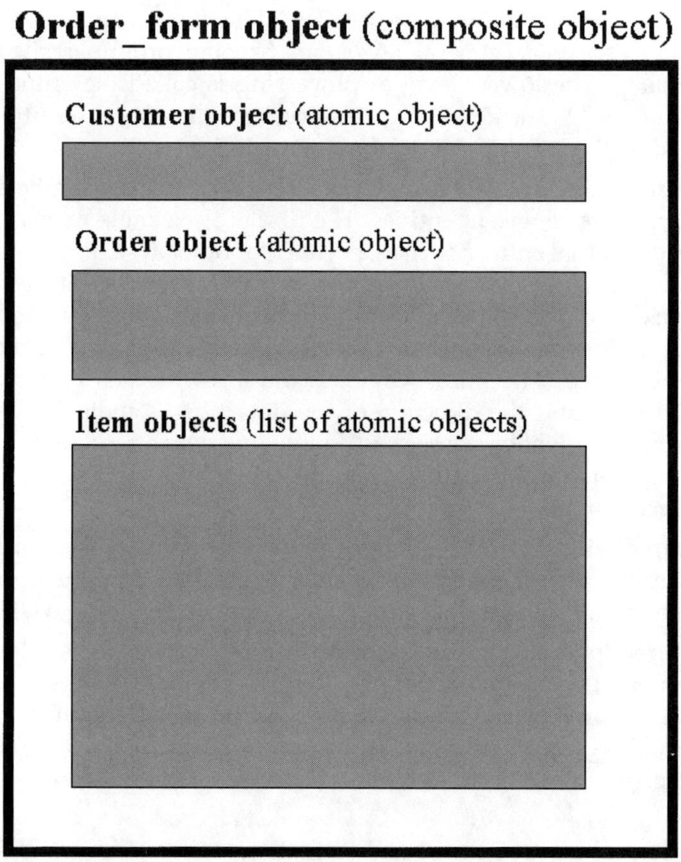

Order_form object (composite object)

Customer object (atomic object)

Order object (atomic object)

Item objects (list of atomic objects)

Figure 3.3   A composite object and its object sub-objects.

Each person sees the real world from a framework of their own personal experiences, and each person's conceptual framework determines how they look at the world around them. Experienced systems individuals are accustomed to viewing databases as being populated with rows, columns, and fields. The object-oriented database analyst must learn to view the world at a much higher level, viewing "objects" as consolidations of many columns and rows, thereby doing a much better job at modeling the real world.

Conceptualization allows a person to look at an object and see new applications for it. This "conceptual reversal" is used by many creative thinkers when they come up with novel uses for existing principles. For example, many people look at an empty soda pop bottle and just see something to be recycled, while others look at it and see a possible bird feeder, vase, or plant holder.

Concepts allow us to develop recognition about the classification of objects. For example, most people use the concept of "wings" to classify airplanes, and the concept of "hull" to identify ships. But what happens when an object such as the Alberta Clipper, the famous seaplane, crosses the conceptual boundaries of two object classes? Sharing characteristics from two concepts, the Alberta Clipper inherits the behaviors and attributes of both aircraft and ships.

It is important to realize that concepts are not required to have any physical existence. Object-oriented systems allow for the use of "abstract", or intangible classes which do not have any concrete objects. The idea of conceptualization can be directly applied to object-oriented database analysis. The primary goal of object-oriented database analysis is to identify the behaviors, some of which may be abstract and the data that may be non-quantifiable. If the goal of object-oriented databases is to closely model the real world, then both concrete and abstract data as well as behaviors must be accounted for in the database analysis.

Object-oriented analysis (OOA) requires the designer to identify the relevant entities, all relationships between these entities, and a generalization hierarchy which decomposes the entities into subclasses. This involves developing a conceptual framework for the system; the perception of the system analyst can have a immense impact on the final design.

In a traditional systems development project, a *structured* specification is prepared to logically describe the hierarchy of processes, the data flowing between processes, and the functionality of each process. The structured specification document provides a complete identification of the system components from a logical perspective.

Object-oriented analysis has the goal of delineating the objects, determining the relationships between the objects, and understanding the behaviors of each object. Whereas a traditional analysis is focused on the transformation of data, object-oriented analysis has a focus on the encapsulation of objects behaviors and the interactions between the objects. This method is an extension of traditional analysis techniques, and begins with a structured specification.

Object-Oriented Analysis

Object-oriented analysis starts with a traditional structured specification and adds the following information:

- **A list of all objects** — A list describing the data contents of each *noun*, or physical entity in the DFD.
- **A list all system behaviors** — A list of all *verbs* within the process; names such as Prepare order summary report, *generate* invoices, etc.
- **A list associating the primary behaviors (services) with each object** — Each object will have behaviors which uniquely belong to the object. Other objects may request the behavior of the object.
- **A description of the contracts in the system** — A *contract* is an agreement between two objects, such that one object will invoke the services of the other.
- **A behavior script for each object** — A *script* describes each initiator, action, participant, and service.
- **A classification for each object and the object relationships** — Generate an entity/relationship model and a generalization hierarchy (IS-A) for each object, using traditional E/R or normalization techniques.

Over the past 12 years, there have numerous books about different approaches to object analysis, but they all contain these common elements. Now that we see the basic analysis requirements, let's explore the basic methodologies for object-oriented analysis.

Different Models for Object Analysis

Unlike the traditional systems analysis where user requirements are gathered and then specifications are put on the requirements and users are then asked to sign-off on the specifications, the object methodologies use a more iterative process where the requirements and specifications are reviewed repeatedly and the users are heavily involved.

Object technology has many different methodologies to help analyze and design computer systems. We will review four of the more popular systems: Rumbaugh, Booch, Coad-Yourdon, and Shlaer-Mellor. In most cases these methodologies are very similar, but each has its own way to graphically represent the entities. To understand and use these four methodologies would become difficult, if not impossible, for all projects. If need be, it is possible to use concepts from one method with concepts from another technique, basically creating your own object development technique. The most important point to remember is that the final outcome is what really matters, not the choice of one analysis technique over another technique. Remember, it is more important to do proper analysis and design to meet user requirements than it is to blindly follow meaningless procedures.

The traditional systems development approach is sometimes referred to as the waterfall method. By waterfall, object analyst's follow a logical progression through analysis, design, coding, testing, and maintenance. Unfortunately, system development seldom fits this kind of structured approach. End-users are notorious for changing their minds or identifying some feature that they forgot to identify. These changes in requirements can happen at any phase of system development and the analyst must struggle to accommodate these changes into the system. What it means for the systems analyst is that you have to go back to whatever step in the development life cycle and make the necessary changes that will then cascade these changes through the entire system. For example, suppose that our end-users are in the testing phase when they realize that they need an additional screen. This would require a change to the initial requirements document, which would, in turn, cascade to analysis, design, and so on.

The object-oriented methodologies require a more iterative process with the same five steps. The iterative process either adds new or more clearly defines existing properties, unlike the traditional approach that would rehash specifications that are already done. The iterative process helps to reduce confusion around what the system is really suppose to do and what the users really want. The object-oriented software development methods make the assumption that user requirements will change, however it doesn't matter which programming language you use—FORTRAN or C++. Irregardless of the system development technique you choose, you will still need to follow the same five steps in system development. It is how these five steps are applied that will make the difference in your system development project.

The Rumbaugh Method

The Rumbaugh method is listed first because it is this author's favorite — it is a very friendly and easy methodology. For traditional system analyst's, the Rumbaugh methodology is the closest to the traditional approach to system analysis and design, and beginners will recognize familiar symbols and techniques. The Rumbaugh method has its primary strength in object analysis but it also does an excellent job with object design. Rumbaugh has three deliverables to the object analysis phase: the Object model, the Dynamic model, and the Functional model. These three models are similar to traditional system analysis, with the additions for the object model, including definitions of classes along with the classes variables and behaviors. The Rumbaugh object model is very much like an entity relationship diagram except that there are now behaviors in the diagram and class hierarchies. The dynamic model is a "state transition" diagram that shows how an entity changes from one state to another state. The functional model is the equivalent of the familiar data flow diagrams from a traditional systems analysis.

The Booch Method

Booch's methodology has its primary strength in the object system design. Grady Booch has included in his methodology a requirements analysis that is similar to a traditional requirements analysis, as well as a domain analysis phase. Booch's object system design method has four parts: the logical structure design where the class hierarchies are defined, the physical structure diagram where the object methods are described. In addition, Booch defines the dynamics of classes in a fashion very similar to the Rumbaugh method, as well as an analysis of the dynamics of object instances, where he describes how an object may change state.

The Coad-Yourdon Method

The Coad-Yourdon method has its primary strength in system analysis. This methodology is based on a technique called "SOSAS", which stands for the five steps that help make up the analysis part of their methodology. The first step in system analysis is called "Subjects", which are basically data flow diagrams for objects. The second step is called "Objects", where they identify the object classes and the class hierarchies. The third step is called "Structures", where they decompose structures into two types, classification structures and composition structures. Classification structures handle the inheritance connection between related classes, while composition structures handle all of the other connections among classes. The next step in analysis is called "Attributes", and the final step is called "Services", where all of the behaviors or methods for each class are identified.

Following analysis, Coad and Yourdon define four steps that comprise the design part of their methodology:

1. **The problem domain component** — defines the classes that should be in the problem domain.
2. **The human interaction component** — defines the interface classes between objects.
3. **The task management component** — identifies system-wide management classes.
4. **The data management component** — identifies the classes needed for database access methods.

The Shlaer-Mellor Method

Shlaer-Mellor methodology has its primary strength in system design and is considered somewhat weak on analysis. The Shlaer-Mellor methodology includes three models: the information model, the state model, and the process model. The information model contains objects, variables, and all the relationships between the objects, and is basically a data model for the system. The state model records the different states of objects and changes that can occur between the objects. The process model is really not much more than a traditional data flow diagram.

Now that we have covered the basics of the object approach, let's take a look at how a real-world object is created by using these techniques.

Creating the Object Model

The object model is one of the three models that is used to describe the complete logical processing in the system. The object model will include the basic object elements, the objects behaviors (methods), the data attributes (variables), and how one object relates to another object. The object model is essentially a graphical roadmap for the system and is an extremely useful tool for both the developers as well as the end-user community. (Figure 3.4) An object's behaviors and variables are listed inside the object boxes, and the object relationships with other objects are designated by the lines connecting the boxes. The object model can be extremely helpful when questions or concerns arise, because you can visually see the design for the system and how the system is constructed.

The object model is a close cousin of the entity/relationship diagram. In fact, the object model is sometimes referred to as an entity/relationship model with the additional constructs of classes and behaviors. In this example, we will use the object model notation of James Rumbaugh, since these authors find it to be one of the most functional object model diagrams. Another feature of the Rumbaugh method is that the object model is more generally associated with design, not analysis, so experienced analysts may find it strange to see this document as part of the analysis phase of systems development.

For example, if we are trying to develop an ordering system for a business it might look like the object model in Figure 3.4. This figure is an object model for Earl's Engines, a small manufacturer of engines for riding-lawn mowers.

Let's examine the meaning of the symbols in Rumbaugh's object model diagram. Starting with the rectangles, the rectangle contains three areas; the class name, the data attributes in the class, and the methods that participate in the class.

The core of the object model are the class entities. For Earl's Engines, we see the both the base classes as well as the subclasses for the model. The base classes include line-item, order, customer, invoice, and item. The subclasses include preferred, international, air_cooled, and water_cooled. As we might guess, the line-item data attributes would be Item number, Item name, Quantity, and Price. The class behaviors follow the class attributes,

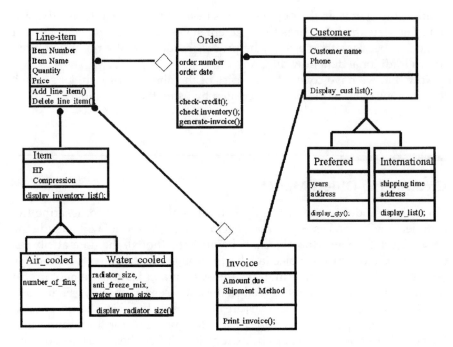

Figure 3.4   A Rumbaugh object model for an order processing system.

and we see that in the line-item class they are listed as add_line_item(), and delete_line_item().

Let's examining the nature of the lines that connect the objects. The dark circles seen on the lines represent the many side of a one-to-many relationship. For example, we see that there is a one-to-many relationship between a customer and an order, since a customer may place many orders, but each order belongs to only one customer. The diamond-shaped symbols represent aggregation. For example, we see that an order is an aggregation of many line items. Finally, we see the triangle-shaped junction that represent subclasses. For example, we see that a customer has two subclasses, one for preferred customers and another for international customers. These subclasses are used to show the new data items and methods that are unique to the subclass.

Let's take a closer look at aggregation. For example, the order-request entity is an aggregate entity made up of many line-items, but each line_item has only one order. The diamond symbol seen on the invoice class and the object_request class is used to denote an aggregation of a number of things (aggregations are sometimes referred to as collections, or assembles). Here we see that an order object is made up of an aggregation of many line-items plus one customer object. An invoice is an aggregation of many line-items plus one customer object.

Note that we are deliberately using the terms "class" and "entity" interchangeably. To the object model they both denote a definition of an object, and the reader should become accustomed to these synonymous terms.

The object model for Earl's Engines also represents IS-A class hierarchies between classes. We use the term IS-A because that is how we specify the participation option of subclasses. For example, a Dodge minivan IS-A van, a van IS-A car, and a car IS-A vehicle. For Earl the customer class has two subclasses, a preferred_customer and an international_customer, each with their own data and behaviors, such that a preferred customer IS-A customer and a international customer IS-A customer. We also see a class hierarchy in the item object, where we see air_cooled and water_cooled subtypes for the item class.

In short, the object model describes all of the relationships between entities, the class hierarchies that exist for each entity and the methods for each class. Now let's move on to see how the dynamic model works with the object model to provide a more complete description of this system.

The Dynamic Model

The dynamic model will show how objects interact with each other and change their "state." A state is defined as a change in an object's values. Unlike the object model that dealt with the static environment of the system, the dynamic model deals with the dynamics of the system and illustrates how the changes to object values are controlled. The dynamic model deals with the events that transpire within the system how an object's variables will change as a result of these events. Basically what we are describing here is what the "state" of an object will be after some event takes place, and this is why the dynamic model is sometimes referred to as a "state transition diagram." In the dynamic model, each class will have a state transition diagram.

For example, if we continue with our ordering system from Figure 3.4 we will examine two sample state transition diagrams: one for the order class and another for the item class (Figure 3.5).

The first example shows how an order may change state from a regular order to either a prepaid order or a COD order. As we can see from this very simple example, the presence of a value in the form_of_payment field will determine the change in state for the order entity.

Looking at the item class in Figure 3.5, we can see that every item has a default value as an in-stock item, but the event of high sales would make the item a back ordered item. However, the event of getting a new shipment of the item would make the item an in-stock item.

The Functional Model

The functional model is the third and final component of the object modeling specification. The functional model shows the processes that are performed within an object and how the data changes as it moves between methods.

Order

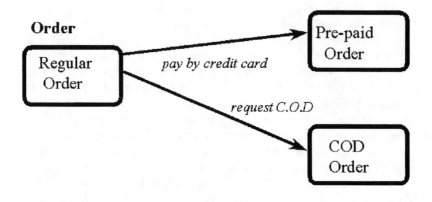

Item

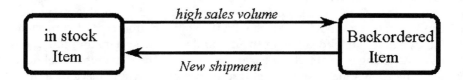

Figure 3.5   A Rumbaugh dynamic model for an order processing system.

Experienced analysts will immediate notice the similarity between the functional model and the traditional data flow diagram. Essentially, Rumbaugh's functional model corresponds to a functional primitive data flow diagram.

The model will show the result of an action, but the model will not display the details on how the action is performed. Again, like the object and dynamic models, the functional model is a visual display of processes and the path of data within the system. To continue with our ordering system example we describe the processes involved in placing an order. (Figure 3.6).

The material in Figure 3.6 describes the internal processing that is done when a customer places an order. When a customer fills out an order form, the system will check the customer's credit by going to the credit history data store and return the customer's credit history. If the customer has bad credit then the order will be rejected. However, if the customer has approved credit then the system will "loop" through each item in the order, checking inventory levels for each item. If the items are in stock then the order will be filled and out of stock items are immediately back-ordered. The system will then go to the inventory data store and subtract the item quantities that were

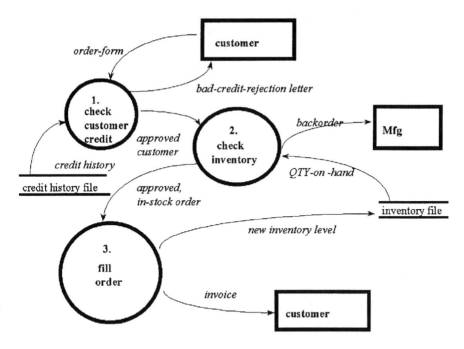

Figure 3.6 A Rumbaugh functional model for an order processing system.

shipped from inventory. The system will also create an invoice that will be sent to the customer with the order.

Summary of Object Analysis

This section should give the reader a feeling for the approaches that are taken to describe the basic logical functionality of their systems. Once the logical model has been created and validated, the developer will then move on to show the physical details of the model. Remember the polestar of systems development; analysis is concerned with the logical model, the design is concerned with the physical representation of the model.

Object Database Design

There is still a great deal of controversy about the best way to approach database design for object-oriented systems. Architecturally, some experts argue that the relational model is not well suited for use in an object-oriented environment while other experts maintain that relational architectures are more suitable for traditional data processing. This has been borne out in the marketplace where we see object-oriented databases used for non-traditional applications such as telephone billing system, while the relational model enjoys predominance in business administration applications.

It is important to recognize that many of the "pure" object-oriented database management systems do not exploit many of the features of "classical" database management. To some object-based systems, the only purpose of an object database (OODBMS) is to provide "object persistence" and very little attention is paid to concurrency-control, rollback and recovery, and the other features associated with relational database management.

One very important point: A database does not have to support all of the formal constructs of the object-oriented approach to benefit from using the object-oriented approach. For example, while object-oriented programming languages such as C++ allow for the creation of abstract data types, the data types offered in most commercial database systems such as, CHAR, INTEGER, REAL, VARCHAR, and BIT are sufficient for almost all database applications.

However, the relational vendors recognize the shortcomings of their architecture. For example, almost every commercial relational database vendor has promised to deliver user-defined data types in their future releases. Oracle, the popular relational database for midrange computers, has announced that Oracle version 8 will support abstract data typing. This topic is fully discussed in Chapter 5, "Relational Database Objects and User-Defined Data Types."

One must remember that the main differences between object-oriented and traditional systems is the idea that in an object-oriented system both data and behavior are stored in the DBMS. In an object-oriented database, instances of a class may behave differently depending upon the processing circumstances. Consider a simple example of how an object-oriented database may differ from traditional systems.

In a traditional database system, all instances of an order record would share the same data items and processing characteristics. Under object-oriented databases, an order will contain not only the order record itself, but the relevant behaviors that are associated with the order. For example, there may be "rush" orders that exhibit different behaviors than would a "COD" order.

Now that we understand the basic precepts of object database design, let's take a look at the major approaches to adding physical details to the logical object model.

Top-down vs. Bottom-up Object Database Design

There are two approaches for developing any database: the top-down method and the bottom-up method. While these approaches appear radically different, they share the common goal of uniting a system by describing all of the interaction between the processes. Let's examine each approach further.

The Top-down Method starts from the general and moves to the specific. Basically, you start with a general idea of what is needed for the system and then ask the end-users what data they need to store. The analyst will then work with the users to determine what data should be kept in the database. Using the top-down method requires that the analyst has a detailed understanding of the system. The top-down method also can have shortcomings. In some cases, top-down design can lead to unsatisfactory results because the analyst and end-users can miss something that is important and is necessary for the system.

The Bottom-up Approach begins with the specific details and moves up to the general. To begin a bottom-up design, the system analyst will inspect all the interfaces that the system has, checking reports, screens, and forms. The analyst will work backwards through the system to determine what data should be stored in the database.

To understand the differences between these approaches, let's consider some jobs that are bottom-up in nature. In statistical analysis, analysts are taught to take a sample from a small population and then infer the results to the overall population. Physicians are also trained in the bottom-up approach. Doctors examine specific symptoms and then infer the general disease that causes the symptoms.

An example of jobs requiring the top-down approach include project management and engineering tasks where the overall requirements must be specified before the detail can be understood. For example, an automobile manufacturer must follow a top-down approach to meet the overall specifications for the car; e.g., that it costs less than $15,000, gets 25 mpg, and seats five people. In order to meet these requirements, the designers must start by creating a specification document and then drill down to meet these requirements.

The analyst will have no choice but to talk to and work with the users to determine what is important to them and as a result determines what data should be stored in the database. What the analyst usually does is to create some prototype reports, screens, and forms to help the users visualize what the system will look like and how it will work.

The Chen Diagram

The basic Chen diagram is the original entity relationship diagram, developed by Peter Chen in 1976.* The diagram is a graphical representation of entities and their relationships to each other. (Figure 3.7) An entity defines a person, place, thing, event or role that you want to keep data about. In the entity relationship diagram an entity is represented by a rectangle. A relationship is an association between two entities, a relationship is represented in the diagram by a diamond. The third part of the entity relationship diagram is called cardinality. Cardinality refers to the number of instances of one

---

* Peter Chen, "The Entity Relationship Model, Toward a Unified View of Data," *ACM Transactions on Database Systems 1* (March 1976), pp. 9–36.

entity that can be related to an instance of another entity. Cardinality can be one to many (1,N), or many to many (M,N) or recursive many-to-many relationships.

In our sample diagram we see a one-to-many relationship between customer and order such that one customer may place many orders, but each order will belong to only one customer. We also see a many-to-many relationship between order and item, such that each order may contain many items, and each item may participate in many orders. Finally, we see a recursive many-to-many relationship, which is defined as an entity that has a many-to-many relationship with itself. For example, an item may have many sub-items, which are items, but are also sub-components in a larger item, e.g., a carburetor has parts, while it is also a part of another item, the engine.

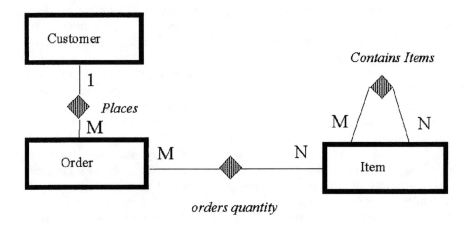

Figure 3.7   A sample Chen diagram.

While the entity/relationship model is very good at describing the overall model for simple data relationships, it is not well suited for object database design. Object design require that physical details be available to the modeler. When contrasted with relational database design, object/relational database design is far more complex. While the relational model dictates that all entities should be decomposed into their smallest components (third normal form), object databases allow far more flexibility in their design. This flexibility translates directly into more complexity for the system designer who must struggle with the huge amount of choices offered by these robust database engines.

Let's begin by exploring the additional structures that are introduced by object-oriented data models and then take a look at a practical diagramming method for object database systems.

Basic Object Data Structures

In addition to collecting data types into user-defined data types, many of the object databases allow for the creation of extensions to the base table types. These extensions may be used to embed additional information into an object or they may be used to establish relationships to other objects. In addition, the extensions may be used to create "aggregate" objects that consist entirely of data inside other objects. These data type extensions fall into several categories:

1. Data extensions with user-defined data types
   - lists of repeating data items
   - lists of groups of repeating data items
2. Pointer extensions to data types
   - single pointers to other rows
   - lists of pointers to other rows
   - lists of pointers to pointers to other rows
   - a pointer to another whole table
   - list of pointers to other whole tables.

As we can see, there is a mind-boggling array of choices of data structures. There are, however, certain rules that the database designer can follow when choosing a data structure to implement within their model. While each of these methods are fully discussed in Chapters 5-8, let's begin our journey by examing just how these data structures are represented graphically in our design documentation.

A Data Representation Model for Object/Relational Systems

One of the confounding problems with the object-oriented extensions to the relational database is the issue of representing the data structures in a graphic form. While early efforts by modeling diagrams have achieved limited success, this approach aspires to display the components of an object/relational database in a simple, easy to understand format. This diagram technique was developed by Don Burleson, a leading object/relational database expert (and author of this book) out of necessity to create a consistent method for documenting object-oriented data models. Let's take a look at some of the components of the model as shown in Figure 3.8.

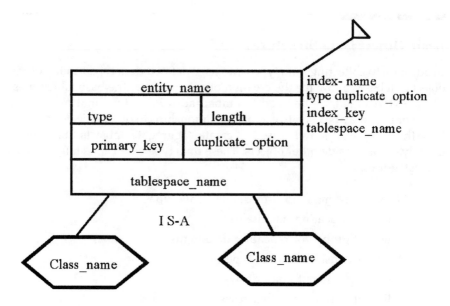

Figure 3.8   A description of the icons in the object/relational diagram model.

Entity Icon Description

This portion of the diagram is the rectangle symbol. Inside the rectangle we provide for the description of all base entities in the data model. Information includes the entity name, the length of the data in the entity, the primary key for the object and whether duplicate keys are allowed, and the place where the object is stored (usually a tablespace for object/relational databases).

The domain values for each entity symbol follow:

Entity_name = This is the internal name of the entity as it appears inside the database.

Type = An entity may be either a table, an OID table, a store table, a view, or an aggregate object.

    Table — This is a generic table as defined within any relational DBMS.

    View — This is a traditional relational view. A view in most relational databases is stored internally as an SQL statement that joins base tables together to form aggregate views of table data. As such a View and an Aggregate table are very similar in purpose.

    OID table — This is an object/relational table which has been defined to contain a special column to contain the object ID for each row in the table.

`Store Table` — A store table is an internal representation of a table whereby an owner table may be coupled with another internal table. For more information on this concept, see Chapter 6, "Relational database objects and reference pointers."

`Aggregate Table` — An aggregate table is a table that represents assemblies of base level objects. These tables are usually made up exclusively of pointers to other OID tables within the model.

`Length` — This is the physical stored length of each row of the entity within the table.

`Primary_key` — This is the column or OID that may be used to uniquely identify each row within the entity.

`Duplicate_Option` — This describes whether duplicate rows are allowed within the entity. Valid values are DN for duplicates not allowed and DA for duplicates allowed.

`Tablespace_Name` — This parameter describes the tablespace where the entity resides inside the database.

Index Descriptions

An index is represented as a line emanating from the entity rectangle, with a triangle at the end of the line. This construct describes all of the information about an index. These items include the name of the index, the type of the index (b-tree or bitmapped), keys for the index, and the place where the physical index is stored.

`Index_name` — This is the internal index name as defined within the database management system.

`Type` — This can have the value of TREE for a B-Tree index or BITMAP for a bitmap structure index.

`Duplicate_Option` — This describes whether duplicate rows are allowed within the index. Valid values are DN for duplicates not allowed and DA for duplicates allowed.

This is explained above

`Key_name` — This contains the names of each column within the entity that participates within the index as a key column.

`Tablespace_Name` — This parameter describes the tablespace where the entity resides inside the database.

Class Descriptions

This component of the model uses polygons to represent that an entity has an attached class hierarchy. While each class name is represented on the diagram, another diagram is used to describe the details about each class hierarchy.

Set Information

This includes all information regarding one-to-many relationships between database entities. As we know there are several ways to represent data relationships between entities in the object relation model:

1. **Foreign key relationships** — These relationships are established by embedding the primary key of one table into another table. The primary key that is embedded in the other table becomes a foreign key in the other table. The relationship is established at runtime by using the SQL JOIN statement to relate the tables together. For example, the following set description shows a foreign key set:

   ```
   CUST-ORDER
   FK DN
   cust_ID
   restrict
   ```

   There are several options available when using foreign key relationships. The relationship can be established in an ad-hoc fashion simply by having two matching columns within two tables, or the foreign key relationship can be defined in a more formal ways using reverential integrity (RI).

   When using RI, the database will manage the data relationship and insure that the constraint is complete. At object insertion time, the RI will check to see the a valid owner key exists before allowing new entities into the model. At object deletion time, the RI will allow two options RESTRICT and DELETE. RESTRICT will not allow the owner object to be deleted if it has any member objects. CASCADE will delete all member objects when the owner object is deleted.

2. **Pointers to rows in other tables** — This construct allows for a columns within a table to contain an array of pointers to rows in the member table. Here is an example:

   ```
   salesperson_order
   row pointer to order
   orderList
   ```

   Here we see that the relationship is called salesperson_order and that it is of the row pointer type, containing a list of pointers to order rows. The column name in the salesperson table is called orderList.

3. Pointers to other tables — These are sometimes referred to as pointers to structures. In the object-relational model, these pointers can point to many rows in a subordinate table. Here is an example of this notation:

```
salespersonHistory
pointer to table history_table
salesHistory
```

Figure 3.9 shows a portion of a complete object/relational diagram. Here we see that there are two entities, one for customer and another for order. The customer is a "table" type, while the order entity has been defined as the "OID table" type, meaning that each row contains a unique object identifier.

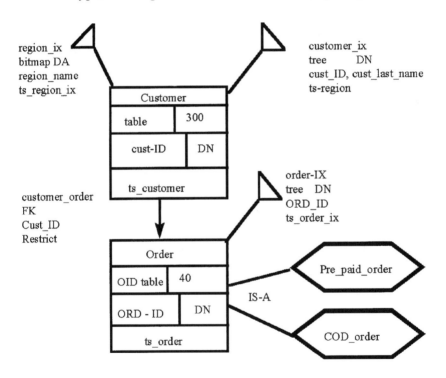

Figure 3.9 A sample object/relational diagram.

Note that there are two indexes on the customer entity. The region_ix index is a bitmapped structure index, which makes sense since a region has only four distinct values. The customer_ix index is a tree index that contains two keys, the cust_ID column, and the cust_last_name column.

Here we also see that the order entity has an attached class hierarchy. As we will learn in detail in later chapters, a class hierarchy contains a "base" class, (which is the order entity in this case). While the order entity will contain all of the base data structures and methods for orders, there are two sub-types of orders, prepaid_order and COD_order, each with their own unique data structures and methods. As we remember from Chapter 1, instantiations of COD_orders and prepaid_orders will inherit the data structures and methods from the order base class.

Summary

Now that we have briefly reviewed the conceptual differences behind the object-oriented extensions to analysis and design, we are ready to delve into the details of the exciting new extensions to the conceptual model for database objects. The following chapter will cover pointers, the uses of inheritance, and the use of methods within the database object model.

4

An Overview of Object Database Standards

The computer industry has been plagued by a lack of standards for decades. As early as the 1960s, we saw that computer hardware and software vendors had a vested interest in keeping their products *proprietary*; that is, non-standard. When most hardware vendors adopted the ASCII character set, IBM steadfastly refused to comply with the standard, and today, computer professionals are still plagued with translating IBMs EBCDIC character set into the ASCII character set used by other hardware.

We see the same parallels in other consumer industry. For example, several years ago a standards war was being fought over a standard format for video tape media. Those who had purchased beta video tapes and equipment learned that the industry was moving to the VHS format and that the beta format was being abandoned. The same is true of electricity. If you travel to another country, you might find that your hair dryer or electric razor will not work, because each country developed standards independently.

This lack of standards is driven by the natural motivation of vendors to keep their products proprietary. Computer hardware vendors have no incentive to make their computers standard, in the sense that they can easily be replaced with other, cheaper computers. We see this trend in the software industry also, where database vendors strive to lock-in their customers so that they will not be able to easily move their processing to other database engines. Imagine what it would be like if other industries failed to develop standards for their products. What it would be like if you could only buy electrical devices from one supplier because you could not mix and match between suppliers?

The same standards issue is true for object technology. The object technology movement has the central goal of making diverse hardware and software interchangeable, in the sense that it would become simple to change hardware and software. In distributed systems, two factions are driving the standards for distributed objects: the Object Management Group's Common Object Request Broker Architecture (CORBA) and Microsoft's Distributed Component Object Model (DCOM).

The Advent of Object Request Brokers

In the early days of object computing, programmers recognized the benefit of having objects within different frameworks communicate with each other. Unfortunately, most objects are tightly coupled with their procedural environment, so it was very difficult for a C++ object to communicate with an object implemented in SmallTalk. This communications problem led the early object programmers to create Object Request Brokers (ORBs) to facilitate communications between objects by providing a middleware layer that would insulate the proprietary nature of the object from the interface (Figure 4.1).

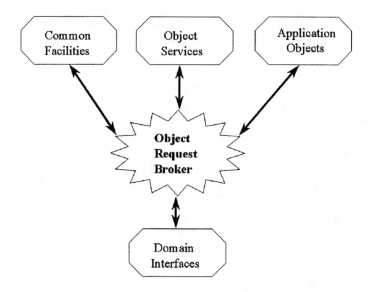

Figure 4.1   An example of an object request broker.

As we can see from Figure 4.1, the ORB communicates with three components. These three components work together to provide a complete application environment. They are:

1. **Application Objects** — The application object interface is a component-based application performing particular tasks for a user. As we know from our discussion of aggregate objects, an application is typically built from a large number of basic objects, and these objects may be nested and combined with other objects to create the database object framework. The ORB is designed to communicate with these application objects, allowing them to pass messages

    to other application objects, or to any of the other object components, such as common facilities or object services.

2. **Domain Interfaces** — Domain interfaces are used to allow for the execution of application-specific functions within the environment, and are generally used to allow communications with diverse hardware and software platforms.

3. **Object Services** — Object services are provided to create objects, to control access to objects, to keep track of relocated objects, and to control the classes of the objects. The purpose of object services is to make a generic environment in which single objects can perform their tasks. The goal of object services is to provide a consistent environment and hopefully improve the reusability of objects across environments.

4. **Common Facilities** — Common facilities are used to provide non-object specific services, such as printing, e-mail, and word processing. Common facilities are generic across the environment, and are shared by all of the users of the ORB.

The idea behind an ORB was to create a framework where they could mix and match language independent objects via a common interface layer. At the lowest level, an ORB is a middleware software component that communicates with objects using a well defined interface protocol. ORBs can also communicate with other ORB's using the same common interface, thereby creating a framework for distributed computing that can span database architectures and hardware platforms.

This is where the Object Management Group entered the picture. In 1991, the OMG produced a specification that standardized the method for writing ORBs called the Common Object Request Broker Architecture, or CORBA. Numerous vendors rushed to develop ORBs that complied with this standard, most notably IBM with their Distributed System Object Model (DSOM).

Despite the early work of the OMG with its CORBA standard, there has been a huge push from Microsoft to dominate the object market. In 1995, Microsoft entered the market with its Component Object Model (COM). Microsoft enhanced COM to include distributed communications in their DCOM model. DCOM has a natural advantage in the ORB marketplace because of its tight integration with the Windows-NT operating system (Figure 4.2).

The DCOM architecture allows for a client object to request an object service from any servers, both local servers as well as remote servers. These object services may take the form of report requests for standard reports and encapsulated data that resides on other servers.

Let's take a look at the details of a DCOM session. When a message or remote procedure call (RPC) is received at a remote host, the stub object acts

OLE Enabled Client

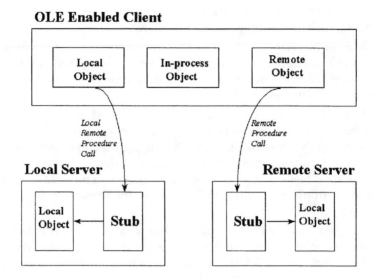

Figure 4.2   The Microsoft DCOM architecture.

as a listener and intercepts the RPC call. The stub objects receives incoming requests and dispatches the request to the appropriate local object on the host. The request is then processed and passed back through the stub object to the originating object.

DCOM has a tremendous advantage over CORBA in that it is already available for use by anyone who is running a Microsoft Windows client. To use DCOM, an application needs only to check with the NT registry to locate the remote ORB, where it can easily invoke a request for services to the remote ORB. For the fast implementation of distributed database objects, Microsoft's DCOM has another natural advantage. It is instantly available without all of the customization that is required when creating a proprietary ORB.

Using an ORB as the central focus for application development is not a new idea. Consider the popular client-server products, Forte and Dynasty. Forte and Dynasty allow the developer to balance the load on their client-server environment by moving process code from the client to the server while the application is running. These products achieve their ability to move process code in a dynamic fashion solely to their use of an internal ORB mechanism.

As a practical matter, the use of ORB-based application development is not very different from traditional application development. For example, consider a University that wants to develop a student management system, with major functional areas including student records, class assignment, and financial aid areas. In a traditional application, the process logic would reside in external application programs, and in an object-oriented environment the process code would reside as methods in a class library.

With a distributed object approach, the process logic would be defined as a part of the ORB. A separate ORB would exist for the student records component, the class management component and the financial aid component (Figure 4.3).

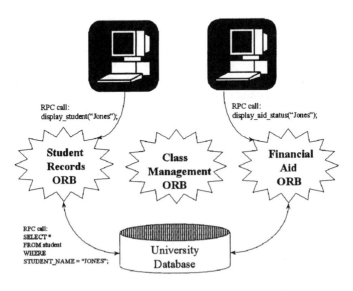

RPC call:
display_student("Jones");

RPC call:
display_aid_status("Jones");

Student Records ORB

Class Management ORB

Financial Aid ORB

RPC call:
SELECT *
FROM student
WHERE
STUDENT_NAME = "JONES";

University Database

Figure 4.3 A sample ORB-based distributed object implementation.

Here we see that the process code would be written in the object definition language (ODL) if we were using CORBA, or in the interface definition language (IDL) if we were using DCOM. Once defined, the ORBs would be instantly accessible to all areas within the computer network that are ORB aware. In the case of Figure 4.3, we see that the client simply requests services from the ORB in the form of an RPC call, and the ORB receives the call and applies the appropriate application logic to make the request to the database, using the database's native access language. The ORB then receives the data, formats the data according to the ORB rules, and returns the data to the requesting client. Note that all of the internal details of both the application logic and the data are hidden from the client.

ORBs and the Internet

In addition to emerging standards for application ORBs, there is a movement in the marketplace to standardize on the implementation of ORB architectures for communications on the World Wide Web.

With the ability to communicate to ORBs on the Internet, Internet clients will be able to instantly communicate with other ORBs on a worldwide basis, making information available from a plethora of data sources. There is a huge movement toward the implementation of distributed objects on the Internet, most notably by the two major Web browser vendors, Microsoft, and Netscape.

Traditionally, using the familiar HTTP protocol (HyperText Transfer Protocol), Netscape has recently announced that it is moving towards an implementation using the CORBA Internet Inter-ORB Protocol (IIOP). The IIOP is rapidly becoming the new protocol for the internet, and is replacing http as a standard method for Web communications.

Microsoft is also looking at providing access to distributed ORBs by using their ActiveX product. Microsoft will link all of their ActiveX objects using a DCE-RPC-enabled communications protocol.

While these efforts are still in their infancy, it is clear that the availability of ORBs on the Internet is not very far away, and that Web surfers will soon be able to make requests for services to ORBs that are distributed on a worldwide basis.

The Object Management Group

The balancing between the vendors drive toward being unique and the industries need to be standard has been addressed with the formation of the Object Management Group. The Object Management Group (OMG) was formed in May of 1989 by Christopher Stone and eight companies to set standards for object technology. These companies included American Airlines, Canon, Data General, Hewlett-Packard, Philips Telecommunications, Sun Microsystems, Unisys Corporation, and 3Com Corporation.

The OMG is committed to developing specifications that are vendor independent, commercially viable, and superior technically for object technology. OMG promotes object technology as a way to allow interoperability and portability, increase productivity, and promote reusability. The OMG has expanded from the original eight companies to over 700 members, only corporate members may submit technology for the OMG to adopt. The OMG headquarters are located in Framingham, Massachusetts.

The main objective of the OMG is interoperability and portability of object technology. This is being driven by end-users who want "plug and play" software — software for both today and tomorrow must be flexible and open so that end-users can change the way their systems are developed and used.

In 1991, the OMG first introduced the Common Object Request Broker Architecture (CORBA) specification. CORBA is concerned with interoperability so that different hardware and software products can communicate with each other. Unfortunately, we still see some pushback from the large software vendors about CORBA. Microsoft has been notably absent in the development of the CORBA standard, and has developed its own approach to system interoperability with DCOM, which is used with Object Linking and Embedding (OLE). While DCOM has been designed to be "largely CORBA compliant,"it still has vendor-specific features that are unique to Microsoft.

Standards and the Object/Relational Databases

Today, we see a real problem in the adoption of standards for database architectures, especially within the domain of the object/relational database vendors. While all of the major database vendors, including Oracle, Sybase, and Informix are touting the availability of CORBA compliant interoperability facilities, there are vast differences between the implementation of their database engines. The new Informix engine, a marriage between the Informix relational database and the Illustra object database, is vastly different from the Oracle8 object/relational database. The Object Database Management group has also failed in the sense that their scope of standards only applies to the "pure" object database engines, and not to the hugely successful mainstream object/relational models.

The ANSI X3H7 committee on object extensions to SQL has also failed in creating standards for object relational SQL, as evidenced by the different implementations of SQL on different databases. While the efforts of the ANSI committees and the OMG are commendable, they have still failed to get the buy-in of some of the database companies. Let's now take a look at how the OMG standards have evolved.

The Object Database Management Group

The haphazard development of standards and definitions of object technology has been very confounding to most companies who are interested in using the new technology. Object technology companies cannot agree on the definition of an object-oriented database, much less the characteristics of an object-oriented database. Many vendor products which are advertised as *object-oriented* capitalize on object technology buzzwords and are often very vague about the real features of the database, and what makes it object-oriented. This is especially true for some of the new object/relational database offerings.

The "pure" object-oriented databases, such as Versant and Objectivity/DB are very powerful tools, but they are tightly coupled to a programming language. Because of their complexity and the high learning curve for using the engines, these types of object-oriented databases have had trouble achieving popularity in the general marketplace.

A new standard for object-oriented database architecture called the ODMG Object Model has been proposed by a consortium of vendors, but the mega-vendors such as IBM and Microsoft have not accepted this standard.

ODMG (Object DataBase Management Group) is a vendor organization which is dedicated to providing standards exclusively for object-oriented databases. The ODMG object model was developed jointly be a consortium of object-oriented database vendors. These companies feel a sense of urgency in creating a unified standard for object-oriented databases, and they have prepared the ODMG model in the hope that all OODBMS vendors will adopt the model. Current commercial OODBMS systems are not portable across hardware platforms, and it is hoped that a joint approach toward object-oriented database architecture will create an environment where object-oriented systems share many characteristics, just as relational databases share common interfaces, such as SQL.

Because of a lack of standards for object-oriented database architectures, most of the major OODBMS vendors have been creating commercial products which have very diverse internal structures.

The ODMG object model was developed jointly by a consortium of object-oriented database vendors, including Versant, Ontos, O2 Technology, Object Design, SunSoft, and Objectivity. Notably absent was Microsoft, which may have decided that its approach to object-oriented database technology didn't fit into the industry standard plan. The companies involved with the ODMG felt a sense of urgency in creating a unified standard for object-oriented databases, and they have prepared the ODMG model in the hope that all OODBMS vendors will adopt the model. But beware, the ODMG database standard was never meant for the object/relational databases such as UniSQL, Oracle8, and Informix. These vendors have had no real standard to guide their efforts.

The ODMG model creates an independent model which is language independent, and object models may be bound to many different languages. ODMG develops a hierarchy of objects with the most general object called a "denotable" object. Denotable objects may be either mutable or immutable. A mutable object may changes its values and properties, but an immutable object contains only literal values.

Within immutable objects, we find two subcategories: atomic and structured (Figure 4.4). A detonable, immutable, atomic object is represented by the same data types found in a relational database, namely CHAR, INTEGER, and FLOAT. A denotable, immutable, structured object is a literal structure such as the DATE and TIME data types.

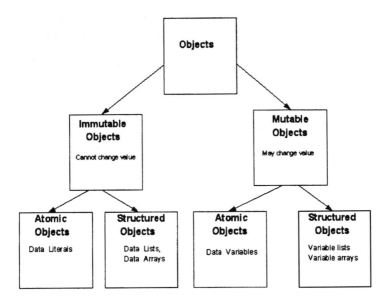

Figure 4.4 The *ODMG-93* database standard.

Unlike the relational database model, the ODMG model requires that all objects are assigned an object identifier (OID), to uniquely identify the object. While it is unclear, it appears that it is not possible to reference an object by the data values in the object. For example, in a relational database one could state: SELECT * FROM ORDER WHERE ORDER_NBR = 456; this would not be possible under this object model. Rather, the ODMG model requires "database currency" to locate the object, and the system must know the OID.

As things stand, the *ODMG93* specification remains in the exclusive domain of the pure object-oriented database vendors. Since the world's leading database vendors have chosen to ignore the ODMG specification in their efforts to objectize their relational engines, it remains to be seem whether the ODMG standard will ever achieve the status of a true industry standard.

Summary

While the emergence of standards for database objects has been making some headway, it is clear that there is still a great deal of work that must be done before all objects will be able to communicate with each other in an independent fashion. As long as vendors have an incentive to keep their products proprietary, we will continue to see resistance in the marketplace, and a failure to develop a uniform methods for interoperability within the database object community.

Now that we have explored the realm of standards, let's move on to take a look at how the object model is being implemented by some of the major database vendors. The following chapters will explore the new object extensions to the database model and describe how these extension are used to develop robust object-oriented applications.

5

Relational Database Objects
and Abstract Data Types

Unlike traditional database management systems which only provide for primitive data types such as INTEGER and CHARACTER, the object-oriented programming languages allow for the creation of abstract data types. The data types offered in commercial database systems—CHAR, INTEGER, NUMBER, VARCHAR, BIT—are sufficient for most relational database applications but developers are now beginning to realize that the ability to create user-defined data types can greatly simplify their database design. While these data types were popular within the programming languages, they have only recently been introduced into the mainstream world of database objects.

Some commercial relational database vendors have committed to incorporating user-defined data type in their future releases. Oracle, the popular relational database for midrange computers, has announced that Oracle Version 8 will support abstract data typing by extending SQL to allow for a CREATE TYPE definition.

At the most basic level, an abstract data type is nothing more than a collection of smaller, basic data types that can be treated as a single entity. While this is a simple concept, the changes in database object design will be dramatic. Some argue that a database must be able to support data types that contain lists rather than finite values, and some of the object/relational databases such as UniSQL allow for a single data type (a column) to contain lists of values, or even another table.

These features are called by several names. In the C programming language, they are called structures; in data structure theory they are called abstract data types (ADTs); and in the marketplace they are referred to as user-defined data types. Each of these terms means essentially the same thing, and we can think of these terms as being interchangeable.

While pre-relational databases supported primitive ADTs, the more robust data typing was not introduced until the object/relational hybrid database became popular. UniSQL, the relational/object-oriented database developed by Dr. Wong Kim, supports the concept of nested tables, whereby a data "field" in a table may be a range of values or an entire table. This concept is called complex, or unstructured data typing. With this approach the domain

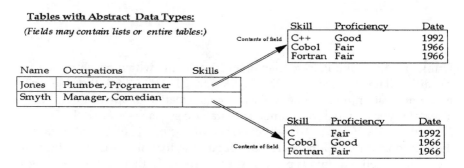

Figure 5.1 An example of embedded complex data types.

of values for a specific field in a relational database may be defined. This ability to "nest" data tables, allows for relationship data to be incorporated directly into the table structure (Figure 5.1). For example, the OCCUPA-TIONS field in the table establishes a one-to-many relationship between employees and their valid occupations. Also, note the ability to nest the entire SKILLS table within a single field. In this example, only valid skills may reside in the SKILLS field, and this implements the relational concept of "domain integrity."

Now that we understand the basic idea behind abstract data types, we can explore some of the compelling benefits to this approach.

Benefits of User-Defined Data Types

It is interesting to note that the ability to represent user-defined data types was commonly used within pre-relational database, and was lost when the relational model was introduced. In pre-relational databases, there were only a small number of allowable data types (numeric and character), but these databases allowed for the atomic values to be grouped into larger units. These larger units could then be easily moved around within the database. For example, a full_address construct could be defined and copied into numerous record definitions, where it could be manipulated as if it were a single unit.

There are several reasons why ADTs are useful within an object database:

1. **Encapsulation:** Because each user-defined data type exists as a complete entity, including the data definitions, default values, and value constraints, this entity insures uniformity and consistency. Once defined, a user-defined data type may participate in many other user-defined data types, such that the same logical data type, always has the same definition, default values, and value constraints, regardless of where it appears in the database.

2. **Reusability:** As a hierarchy of common data structures is assembled, it can be re-used within many definitions, saving coding time and insuring uniformity.

3. **Flexibility:** The ability to create real-world data representations of data allows the database object designer to model the real world as it exists.

As you can see there are many compelling reasons to have user-defined data typing, provided that the data types are properly analyzed and incorporated into the database object model. Let's take a look at some of the implementation issues that relate to the object model and data typing.

Basic User-Defined Data Types

One of the shortcomings of the relational model was the requirement to model all data at their smallest level. For example, if we want to select all of the address information for a customer, we are required to manipulate street_address, city_address, and zip_code as three separate statements. With abstract data typing, we can create a new data type called full_address, and manipulate it as if it were an atomic data type. While this may seem like a huge improvement, it is interesting to note that pre-relational databases supported this construct, and the COBOL language had ways to create data "types" that were composed of sub-types. For example, in COBOL, we could define a full address as follows:

```
05 CUSTOMER-ADDRESS.
   07 STREET-ADDRESS PIC X(80).
   07 CITY-ADDRESS PIC X(80).
   07 ZIP-CODE PIC X(5).
```

We can then move the customer-address as if it were an individual entity:

```
MOVE CUSTOMER-ADDRESS TO PRINT-REC.
MOVE SPACES TO CUSTOMER-ADDRESS.
```

By the same token, an object database will allow the definition of a customer_address data type.

```
CREATE TYPE customer_address (
   street_address char(20),
   city_address char(20),
   state_name char(2)
     CONSTRAINT STATE_NAME IN (CA,NY,IL,GA,FL),
   zip_code number(9)) DEFAULT VALUE 0;
```

It is apparent that the data type definition contains much more than just the data and the data size. We may also assign default values to the data types and specify value constraints. The default value and constraint checks happen at object creation time, and this insures that the database designer has complete control over the data definition as well as the values that are inserted into the data type.

We could then treat customer_address as a valid data type, using it to create tables and select data:

```
CREATE TABLE customer (
    full_name          cust_name,
    full_address       customer_address,
    . . .
    );
```

Now that the table is defined, we can reference full_address in our SQL just as if it were a primitive data type:

```
SELECT DISTINCT full_address FROM CUSTOMER;

INSERT INTO customer VALUES (
    full_name ('ANDREW','S.','BURLESON),
    full_address('123 1st st.','Minot, ND','74635');

UPDATE CUSTOMER (full_address) VALUES ' ';
```

Note that the SQL select statements change when accessing rows that contain user-defined data types. Here is the SQL syntax to select a component of full_address:

```
SELECT full_address.zip_code
FROM customer
WHERE
full_address.zip_code LIKE '144%';
```

Lists of Repeating Data Items

For many years, the idea of repeating data items within an object has been repugnant to database designers. The tenets of data normalization dictated that the removal of repeating data items was the very first step toward a clean data model.

The introduction of lists of values into relational databases was first done by the UniSQL database. At the time, this non-first normal form modeling ability was treated with suspicion as raised the ire of the titans of relationa modeling. However, these repeating groups became more respectable, and even C.J. Date introduced a new concept into the relational model called a "set," to allow this construct to fit into the relational paradigm. Today, we recognize that there are specific instances where the introduction of a repeating group will enhance a database design.

In order to use repeating groups with a design, the following should be true:

1. The data items should be small in size.
2. The data item should be static and rarely changed.
3. The repeating data should never need to be queried as a "set."

To illustrate this principle, consider the following example. Suppose that we are designing a university database and we notice that a student may take the ACT exam up to three times, and our database must capture this information. Without repeating groups, we have two choices:

1. We can create unique columns within our student table, naming each repeating group with a subscript:

```
create table student  (
    sudent_ID              number(5),
    . . .
    act_score_one          number(3),
    act_score_two          number(3),
    act_score_three        number(3))
```

2. We could "normalize" out the repeating groups and move them into another table:

```
create table act_score  (
    student_ID             number(5),
    act_score              number(3));
```

Now, let's take a look at how the repeating group might be implemented:

```
CREATE TYPE act_type as VARRAY(3) OF act_score;
```

Here we see that we have defined a data structure that can use an implied subscript to reference the data. For example, to insert the test scores for Robin Haden, we could enter:

```
INSERT INTO
            student
        act_score(
                        VALUES
                        500
                        556
                        621)
    WHERE
        student_last_name = Haden;
```

Now to select the test score for Robin Haden, we could query the act_scores by referring to the subscript:

```
SELECT
            act_score(1),
            act_score(2),
            act_score(3)
    FROM
            student
    WHERE
    student_last_name = Haden;
```

Now that we understand the concept of repeating values within a database object or a relational table and the object-oriented extensions to SQL to handle these structures, let's take a look at the advantages and disadvantages of this approach.

The primary advantages to repeating groups are immediately available when the object or row is fetched. Less disk space is consumed, since we do not have to create another table to hold the act scores. Remember, if we create another table, we will need to redundantly duplicate the student_ID for each and every row of the act_score table.

The main disadvantage of repeating groups is that they cannot easily be queried as a distinct set of values. In other words, we would not be able to query to see all students who have received an ACT score greater than 500.

```
DECLARE c1 AS CURSOR FOR
    SELECT * FROM STUDENT;

FOR score IN c1
LOOP

    Fetch c1 into :score;

    FOR i = 1 to 3
    LOOP
        IF act_score(i) > 500
        THEN
            PRINT student_name
        END IF
    END LOOP
END LOOP
```

Another alternative to using a cursor would be to use the SQL union operator. As you can see, this involves creating a temporary table to hold all of the values into a single column.

```
CREATE TABLE TEMP as
(
SELECT act_score(1) FROM student
  UNION
SELECT act_score(1) FROM student
UNION
SELECT act_score(1) FROM student
)
SELECT act_score
FROM temp
WHERE act_score > 500;
```

On the other hand, if we were to remove the repeating group of act_scores and place them in a table called act_score, we could then query the table to easily get the list of students:

```
SELECT student_name
FROM student, act_score
```

```
WHERE
    act_score.stident_ID = student.student_ID
    AND
    act_score > 500;
```

One other confounding problem with repeating groups within objects is that we do not know in advance how many cells will contain data. Therefore, we would need to test to see how many of the values are present. Special code must be added to test whether the column is NULL as shown in the following example:

```
FOR i - 1 to 3
LOOP
    IF act_score(i) IS NOT NULL
    then
    . . .
END LOOP
```

Nesting of User-Defined Data Types

Now let's take this concept one step further and consider how user-defined data types can be nested within other data types. A basic example, would be to create a data type that would encapsulate all of the data in a table:

```
CREATE TYPE    customer_stuff (
    full_name              customer_name,
    home_address           customer_address
    business_address       customer_address);
```

With the customer_stuff type defined, table definition becomes simple:

```
CREATE ABLE CUSTOMER (customer_data      customer_stuff);
```

Using this type of user-defined data type we are essentially duplicating the object-oriented concept of encapsulation. That is, we are placing groups of related data types into a container that is completely self-contained and has the full authority of the innate relational data types such as int and char.

```
Select customer_stuff.customer_name.zip_code
   from customer
where customer_stuff.customer_name.zip_code like
   144%;
```

Displaying Abstract Data Types with SQL

But there is to abstract data types than the ability to define them within a relational table. Another useful feature of these data types is to be able to reference then from within an SQL query. Since data types are normally comprised of sub-parts, the SQL must be extended to allow for the entire data type to be referenced as a single unit, while the SQL will automatically format all of the sub-components. For example, the following SQL would display full_address data without the need to select each sub-type:

```
SELECT DISTINCT full_address FROM CUSTOMER;
```

This SQL would produce a listing like this:

STREET_ADDRESS	CITY_NAME	STATE_ABBR	ZIP_CODE
123 First Street	Minot		ND37363
44 West Avenue	Albuquerque	NM	77112
8337 Glenwood Drive	Fairport	NY	14450
3 Wedgewood Avenue	Denver		CO63533

Note that we would also have to alter our SQL if we wanted to select a component of full_address. This is generally done by specifying the sub-component by inserting a "dot" between the higher-level data type and the data item that we wish to display:

```
SELECT full_address.street_address
WHERE
full_address.zip_code LIKE '144%';
```

This would produce the following listing:

```
STREET_ADDRESS
8337 Glenwood Drive
```

Now that we understand how ANSI standard SQL has been extended for selecting rows that contain abstract data types, lets move on to look at how abstract data types are updated with SQL.

Updating Abstract Data Types with SQL

Since user-defined data types contain sub-entities, special extensions will need to be added to relational SQL to allow for these aggregate data types to be updated. This would involve partitioning the SQL UPDATE statement to allow for the sub-types to be specified. For example, the SQL to update a customer address might look like this:

```
UPDATE  CUSTOMER
        (full_address
            (
            VALUES  (
                               '444  North  Avenue',
                               West  Lake
                               NJ
                               83733
                               )

            )
        );
```

As we see from this example, the update statement is referencing only the full_address data type, but since it consists of sub-types, we must specify each of the sub-types separately in the update statement.

Nesting of Abstract Data Types

Now let's take this concept one step further and consider how to nest abstract data types within other data types. Remember, the primary reason for the introduction of user-defined data types is the ability to reuse these components in a consistent fashion across the entire database domain. Since data types are created to encapsulate other data types we should be able to "nest" or embed user-defined data types within other user-defined data types. For example, we could create a data type that would encapsulate all of the data in a table, and then use this data type in a table definition:

```
CREATE TYPE     customer_stuff (
    full_name           customer_name,
    home_address        customer_address
    business_address    customer_address);
```

With the customer_stuff type defined, table definition becomes simple:

```
CREATE TABLE CUSTOMER (customer_data     customer_stuff);
```

By using this type of user-defined data typing we are essentially duplicating the object-oriented concept of encapsulation. That is, we are placing groups of related data types into a container that is completely self-contained and has the full authority of the innate relational data types such as int and char.

Displaying nested user-defined data types would be performed in the same fashion as the earlier sample queries with the exception that the target data types would require several "dots" to delimit the levels of nesting within the data structure. For example, the following query will display the street_address for a customer.

```
Select customer_stuff.customer_name.zip_code
    from customer
where customer_stuff.customer_name.zip_code like
    144%;
```

Here we see that a reference to zip_code must be prefaced with customer_name since it participates in this data types. Further, the customer_name data type is nested within the customer_stuff data types. Hence, the proper SQL reference to zip_code is expressed as customer_stuff.customer_name.zip_code.

Now, let's move on to take a look at how data type usage is managed.

Displaying Data Type Usage

In object-oriented data models, the ability to "nest," or embed data definition within other definitions has tremendous benefits for the database administrators who must manage the data definitions. In pre-relational databases it was possible to see "where-used" information for any data item in the enterprise.

A bill-of-material relationship existed in the data dictionary to relate both the sub-data items of a data type as well as the higher-level components where the data items is used. Also, since each any every method is now stored in the database, it is possible to see where a data item is referenced. For some relational databases that still allow external programs, the database pre-compiler will record all external programs that reference the data type. Hence, user-defined data types with a robust dictionary will allow the DBA to see every place where a data type is used so that they can identify every place where a data definition needs to be changed.

For example, consider the following data dictionary report for our full_address datatype:

```
Full_address data type
```

Consists of:

```
(street_address, city_address, zip_code)
```

Part of:

```
(customer_address, employee_address,
     vendor_address)
```

Used in methods:

```
customer.insert
customer.update
customer.select
customer.produce_mailing_label
employee.insert
employee.update
employee.select
employee.produce_pink_slip
employee.mail_paycheck
vendor.insert
vendor.update
vendor.select
vendor.produce_mailing_label
```

Used in C Programs:

```
PSSC102;
SPSH464
PJUY775
```

In this example listing from a data dictionary, we can see that the data dictionary has provided everything that we need to know about the full_address data type. This can be an extremely useful feature for database objects, especially when data types change their definition. Consider how simple it would be to change a zip code from 5 digits to 9 digits, or change a year field from 2 digits to 4 digits. Every place where the data type exists can be easily identified.

Designing a Hierarchy of Data Types

One of the challenges of abstract data typing is the definition of a hierarchy of related data types. In order to get the benefit of re-usable data structures, it is necessary to define a hierarchy of data types.

As we know by intuition, data types naturally form a recursive many-to-many relationship with other data types, such that a data type may be composed of data types, while at the same time being a part of a larger data type (Figure 5.2).

This relationship has be expressed in a set occurrence diagram, where we can see the linkages between the has_parts and the is_a_part relationship (Figure 5.3). Here we see that the full_address data types has the components, street_address, city_address and zip_code, while at the same time, full_address is cast as the customer_address and the employee_address datatypes, participating in the customer_stuff and the employee_stuff data types.

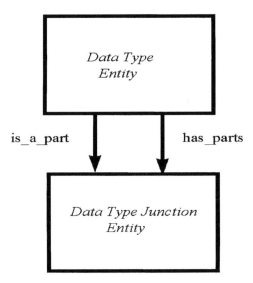

Figure 5.2   A model for a recursive data type hierarchy.

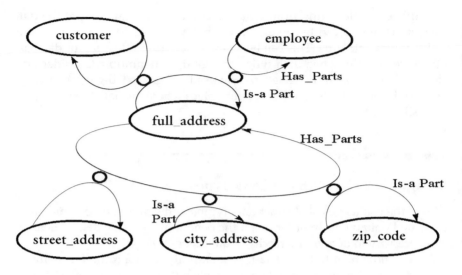

Figure 5.3   A set occurrence diagram for data types.

In the relational model, the relationship between data types is expressed by creating an intersection record to establish the many-to-many relationship (Figure 5.4).

Here we see that the junction table has only two columns: HAS-PARTS and IS-A-PART. By issuing a relational JOIN operation, we can build the data structures for any data item. For example, the following SQL will display all of the components within the full_address datatype. In this example, we join

	Data Type	
Type Table	customer employee full_address street_address city_address zip_code	

	IS-A PART	HAS PART
Component Table	customer employee full_address street_address city_address zip_code	full_address full_address full_address street_address city_address zip_code

Figure 5.4   A tabular representation of data types

using the has_parts relationship to see the sub-components of the full_address:

```
SELECT
    has_part
FROM
    component_table
WHERE
    is_a_part = full_address;

HAS_PART
_____
street_address
city_address
zip_code
```

Conversely, we can also display where a data type appears as a sub-part in a larger data type. In the following example, we can display where the full_address participates:

```
SELECT
    is_a_part
FROM
    component_table
WHERE
    has_parts = full_address;

IS-A-PART
_____
customer
employee
```

Now that we understand the internal representation of user-defined data types within the databases dictionary, let's move on to take a look at how they are used and manipulated within database methods.

Manipulating ADTs

In many object databases it is possible to directly retrieve and pass an abstract data type. While this is a matter of convenience for most programmers, there are some very useful applications of this technique, especially for the object/relational databases. In object/relational databases, ADTs can be directly retrieved and used inside other tables. In the following Oracle example, a new table called good_customer is created by retrieving the entire ADT from the customer table.

```
create table good_customer as
(select value(a) from customer a where type = good)
```

In this example, the good_customer table will inherit the same ADT as the customer table.

Another feature of abstract data typing is the simplification of the transfer of data structures between the database and the front-ends. In a traditional relational database, each column has to be moved, one at a time, from the database into the map field for the display screen. In the following example, we see the C syntax to move data onto a display screen:

```
strcpy(db_cust_first_name,screen_cust_first_name);
strcpy(db_cust_last_name,screen_cust_last_name);
strcpy(db_cust_MI,screen_cust_MI);

strcpy(db_cust_street_address,screen_cust_street_
    address);
strcpy(db_cust_city,screen_cust_city);
strcpy(db_cust_zip_code,screen_cust_zip_code);
```

When using an ADT, a single statement can be used to transfer the data from the database onto the display screen:

```
strcpy(db_customer_struct, screen_customer_struct);
```

Summary

Now that we have a general understanding of the function and operation of abstract data types within the database object model, we can now move to on to more advanced topics. In the following chapters we will introduce pointers to objects, the creation of aggregate objects, and the use of inheritance within the database object model. It is the synergy of all of these features that makes the object-oriented and object/relational database a powerful new addition to the arsenal of systems development tools.

6

Relational Database Objects and Pointers

Before we begin out discussion of pointers, it is important to understand exactly what a pointer represents and how it is implemented in object databases. In pre-relational databases, each record in the database had a distinct address. These addresses were the numbers that corresponded to a physical database block. Also included in the address was the "offset" or displacement of the target record into the block. For example, an address of 665:2 would refer to the second record in database block number 665. Once defined, these addresses could be stored inside other records, essentially allowing one record to point to another record. These pointers became the foundation of establishing relationships between entities in pre-relational times.

For object/relational databases, there is the ability to create a distinct object identifier (OID) to uniquely identify each row within an object/relational table. These OIDs are guaranteed to remain unique by the database software, and like pointers, OIDs can be embedded into columns, providing the ability to point to other rows in the database.

The issue of establishing relationships between data items is not a new concept. As we discussed in Chapter 2, many of the pre-relational databases employed linked-list data structures, which create embedded pointers in the prefix of each occurrence of a database entity. These pointers were used to establish the one-to-many and many-to-many relationships between the entities.

Although the design of the pointer-based databases was very elegant in the sense that foreign keys were not needed to establish data relationships, there were serious problems with implementation. Network databases such as CA-IDMS and hierarchical databases such as IMS are very difficult to navigate because the programmer must be aware of the location, name and types of each pointer in the database.

Even worse, the use of pointers for establishing data relationships makes structural changes a nightmare. Because the data relationships are "hard-linked" with embedded pointers, the addition of a new pointer requires special utility programs to "sweep" each and every effected entity in the database. As each record is located, the prefix of the entity is restructured to accommodate the new pointers. While the "pure" object-oriented databases have this problem of restructuring, the object/relational databases avoid this problem because the SQL ALTER TABLE syntax can be used to add the new pointer column to the entity without restructuring all of the rows in the table.

Database Navigation with Pointers

One major feature of the relational database model is their requirement that rows be addressed by the contents of their data values (with the exception of relational databases that support the ROW_ID construct). Now, within the object/relation model, there will be an alternative access method for rows, such that rows may be identified by either their data values, or by their object IDs (OIDs). For example:

```
SELECT
    customer_stuff
FROM
    customer
WHERE
    customer_ID = 38373;
```

In the object/relational model, we can also use SQL to address rows by their OIDs, thereby allowing pointer-based database navigation:

```
SELECT
    customer_stuff
FROM
    customer
WHERE
    OID = :host_variable;
```

The object-oriented database models as well as the object/relational models require the concept of "currency", so that records may be addressed independently from their data. As we remember from Chapter 2, the CODASYL model supported the declaration of abstract sets to relate classes together, and also supports the notion of currency, whereby a record may be accessed without any reference to the record's data.

This is the core difference between the database architectures. While a pure relational database will rely on the SQL optimizer to retrieve the requested rows from the database, the object-oriented databases and the object/relational databases may "navigate" the database, one entity at a time. As such, these architectures must be able to support navigation, and the programmers must be able to recognize where they are within the database.

A navigational programmer is required to clearly describe the access path that the database will use to service the request. The access path is clearly described in their code, and the programmer can graphically show the path with an object/relational diagram. In SQL however, the access path in not evident and is hidden because the access is determined by the SQL optimizer, usually at run time. The SQL optimizer interrogates the system tables to see if the "target" relational tables have indexes, an then determines the optimal access path to service the SQL request. The SQL optimizer uses several access methods, including sequential scans, sequential pre-fetch, and index scans. Only by running the SQL EXPLAIN utility can the programmer see the access path to the data.

Now that we understand the conceptual history behind the use of pointers in database management, let's move on to take a look at how they are implemented in the object/relational databases. While the "pure" relational model was defined as being devoid of pointers, the new conventional wisdom is to uniquely identify each row in each table, and allow these unique Object Identifiers (OIDs) to be stored within tables, essentially acting as pointers to other relational rows. The following section will examine how this works.

Using Pointer References with Object/Relational Databases

The ability to define data types that contain pointers to rows in other database tables will profoundly change the way that databases are created and maintained. These extensions to the relational model will allow a cell in a table to reference a list of values, or another entire table. This ability allows the designer to define and implement "aggregate objects" that contain pointer references to the components, rather than having to define a relational view on the data. This also allows the database designer to more effectively model the real-world, reduce overhead, and provide a way to attach "methods" or behaviors to aggregate objects.

Repeating Groups and Abstract Data Types

Let's take a look at how repeating values appear in the Oracle object/relational model. The Oracle databases language (called PL/SQL), uses the varying-array language construct (VARRAY) to indicate repeating groups, so we can use the VARRAY mechanism to declare repeating groups within table columns. Let's examine an example. In the following SQL we will add a repeating group called job history to our customer table. First, we create a TYPE called job_history with a maximum of three values:

```
CREATE TYPE          full_name  (
first_name           char(20),
middle_initial       char(1),
last_name            char(20));

CREATE TYPE          full_address  (
street_address       char(20),
city_address         char(20),
state_name           char(2),
zip_code             char(5));

CREATE TYPE          job_details  (
job_dates            char(80),
job_employer_name    char(80),
job_title            char(80)
job_address          full_address);

CREATE TYPE          job_history  (
VARRAY(3) OF REF     job_details);
```

Now that we have defined the data types, here is how we can create the object/relational table using the data types:

```
CREATE TABLE CUSTOMER (
customer_name        full_name,
cust_address         full_address,
prior_jobs           job_history);

CREATE TABLE         JOB_HISTORY (
job_stuff            job_details);
```

Here we see that we have created a repeating list within our table definition (Figure 6.1). In addition to de-referencing the data type, we would also need to subscript the prior_jobs to tell Oracle which one of the repeating items we want to view:

```
SELECT customer.prior_jobs.job_title(3)
FROM CUSTOMER
WHERE
customer.customer_name.last_name LIKE 'JONES%';
```

Here we select the first previous employers street address:

```
SELECT customer.prior_jobs.job_address.street_
    address(1)
FROM CUSTOMER
WHERE
customer.customer_name.last_name LIKE 'JONES%';
```

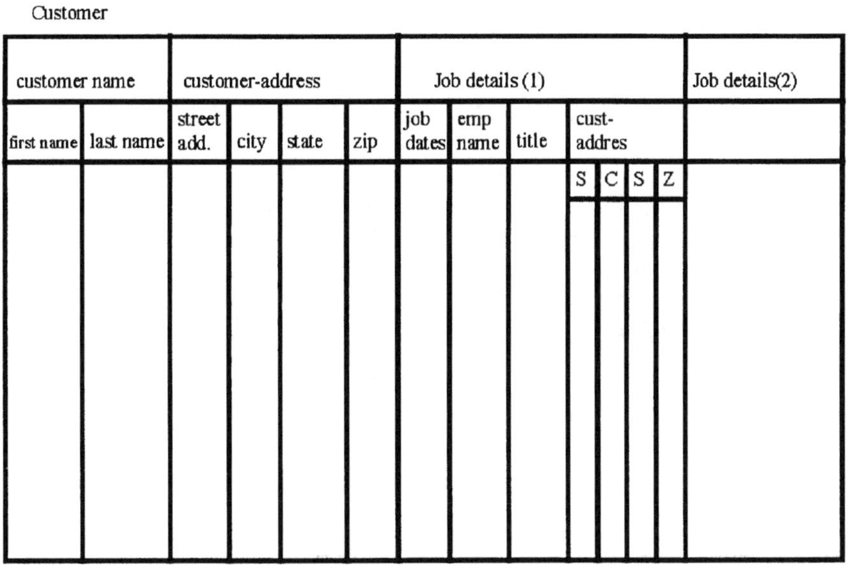

Customer

customer name		customer-address				Job details (1)								Job details(2)
first name	last name	street add.	city	state	zip	job dates	emp name	title	cust-addres					
									S	C	S	Z		

Figure 6.1   A repeating list within a table column.

Note that it is possible in an object/relational database to make the repeating groups contain either data or pointers to rows within other tables. But what happens when we "nest" data types that have repeating groups? In pre-relational databases, it was easy to create a record that contained a finite repeating group. For example, in COBOL a record definition could be defined to contain three repeating groups of job history information:

```
03 EMPLOYEE.
    05 EMPLOYEE-NAME            PIC X(80).
    . . .
    05 JOB-HISTORY OCCURS 3 TIMES.
        07 JOB-DATE             PIC X(80).
        07 JOB-EMPLOYER-NAME    PIC X(80).
```

```
07  JOB-TITLE              PIC  X(80).
07  EMPLOYER-ADDRESS
    09  STREET-ADDRESS  PIC  X(80).
    09  CITY-ADDRESS    PIC  X(80).
    09  ZIP-CODE        PIC  X(80);
```

So, in COBOL, the JOB-HISTORY component can be referenced by a subscript and any component, for example JOB_HISTORY can be referenced by a subscript:

```
MOVE  JOB-HISTORY(2)  TO  OUT-REC.
MOVE  'DATABASE  ADMINISTRATOR'  TO  JOB-TITLE(3).
```

Now, let's take a look at how these repeating values may appear in an object/relational database. As we saw before, we use the VARRAY construct to indicate repeating groups, so it is a safe assumption that a VARRAY mechanism can be used to declare our job history item:

```
CREATE  TYPE  customer_address  (
    street_address      char(20),
    city_address        char(20),
    zip_code            char(5));

CREATE  TYPE  job_details  (
    job_dates           char(80),
    job_employer_name char(80),
    job_title           char(80)
    job_address         customer_address);

CREATE  TYPE  job_history  (
    VARRAY(3)  OF  job_details);
```

Now, look how we can create the CUSTOMER table using the data types that we have just defined:

```
CREATE  TABLE  CUSTOMER  (
    customer_name  full_name,
    cust_address   full_address,
    prior_jobs     job_history);
```

We have created a table with three occurrences of job history details. As we have already seen we need to subscript the prior_jobs to tell the database which one of the three items that we want:

```
SELECT customer.prior_jobs.job_title(3)
FROM  CUSTOMER
WHERE
customer.customer_name.last_name LIKE 'JONES%';
```

Database designers will note that this data structure is a direct violation of first normal form! As you may recall from your college days, one fundamental principle (or restriction, however you want to look at it) was that a relational table could not contain repeating values. This was primarily because SQL had no mechanism to allow for repeating groups to be defined and subscripted. Now that we understand repeating groups within object/relational columns, let's introduce pointers into the model.

Establishing Data Relationships to other Tables with Pointers

We have now violated first normal form and upset Chris Date, let's carry this argument one step further. If it is possible to allow for repeating values within a table cell, why not a reference to an entirely new table? Imaging a database which allows nesting of tables within tables such that a single cell of one table could be a pointer to another whole table. While this concept may seem very foreign on the surface, it is not too hard to understand if we consider that many real-world "things," or objects, are made up of sub-parts.

A special note on pointers: in order to establish data relationships between database entities, a pointer must be persistent, unique, and nonexpiring. In pre-object/relational databases a relational Row ID was used to identify a row. Unfortunately, this Row ID was the number of the physical database block and row displacement within the data block. As such, a relational row could "move" to another block as a result of routine maintenance, or be deleted. To address this problem, the object/relational vendors have devised a way to create OIDs for each row that will always uniquely identify a row, regardless of the row's status. For example, a database row could be deleted, and the OID that was associated with that row will never be reused by the database software.

To create a table with OIDs, a data type must be created that contains all of the necessary row information. In the following example, assume that the data type customer_stuff contains all of the required data structures for a customer table. In a traditional relational databases, we could create the table like this:

```
CREATE TABLE customer (customer_data    customer_stuff);
```

With the introduction of OIDs, the table creation syntax has changed slightly. The following example will create the exact same table as our earlier example, with the exception that the table will contain an OID for each row that is created within the customer table:

```
CREATE TABLE customer OF customer_stuff;
```

It has always been a shortcoming of the relational model that only atomic things could be directly represented, and relational "views" were required to assemble aggregate objects. The object technology professors always used to make fun of the relational model's inability to represent aggregate objects, stating that it would be like disassembling your car each evening when you are done driving it, only to reassemble your car each time that you want to drive it. At last, nested abstract data types allow Oracle users to represent real-world "things" without resorting to views.

Let's take a look at how this type of recursive data relationship might be represented within an object/relational database. The following SQL creates a TYPE definition for a list of orders. This list of pointers to orders might become a column within an Oracle table.

```
CREATE TYPE order_set
  AS TABLE OF order;

CREATE TYPE CUSTOMER_STUFF (
   customer_id             integer,
   customer_full_name      full_name,
   customer_full_address   full_address,
   . . .
   order_list              order_set);

CREATE TABLE customer OF customer_stuff;
```

Here we see the new style of table creation syntax. Both of the following table declarations are identical, except that the CREATE TABLE OF syntax will establish the Object IDs so that other tables may contain references to rows in the customer table.

Without OIDs: CREATE TABLE customer (cust_data
   customer_stuff);
With OIDs: CREATE TABLE customer OF customer_stuff;

Employee Table

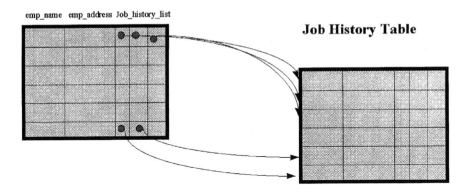

Figure 6.2   Pointers to other database rows.

In either case, we have now defined a pointer column called order_list in the customer table. This pointer will point to a list of pointers. Each cell of this list will contain pointers to rows in the order table (Figure 6.2).

While Figure 6.2 shows the pointer structure as it would look conceptually, the object/relational databases must utilize internal arrays to implement these repeating groups of pointers. In Oracle8, the popular object/relational databases, variable-length arrays are used to represent this structure (Figure 6.3)

Here we have nested a list of pointers within each column, and that each of the cells within a column contain a list of pointers to rows in the order table. Using object-oriented SQL extensions, we can now "pre-join" with the order table to add the three orders for this customer;

```
UPDATE customer
  SET order_list (
    select REF(order) /* this returns the OIDs from
        all order rows */
    from order
    WHERE
    order_date = SYSDATE
    and
    order.customer_ID = (123)
  )
```

Here we see the use of the REF operator, which returns the "reference", or OID of the requested rows. This is similar to the retrieval of Row IDs in a relational database, except that we are now storing the row information inside a relational table.

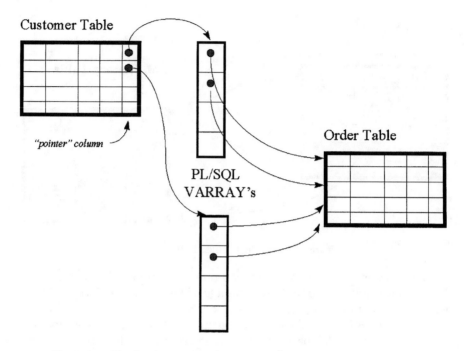

Figure 6.3   The Oracle8 representation of repeating lists of pointers to rows.

Now let's take a look at how we can navigate between tables without having to join tables together. Remember from out earlier discussion, that the object/relational model provides for two ways to retrieve data from our database. We can use SQL to specify the desired data and let the SQL optimizer choose the access path, or we can navigate our database, one row at a time, and gather the required information. Here is how we might access this data using the DEREF extension to SQL.

```
SELECT DEREF(order_list)
from CUSTOMER

where

customer_id = 123; /* this will return 3 rows in
    the order table */
```

The important point in the above example is that we have navigated between tables without ever performing a SQL join. Consider the possibilities. We would NEVER need to embed the foreign key for the customer table in the order record, since we could store the pointers in each customer row. Of course, we would never be able to perform a relational join between the customer and order tables, but this would not really make any difference as long as we have maintained the ability to navigate between customers and orders with pointers.

Of course, these are one-way pointers from customer to orders, and we would not have a method to get from the order table to the customer table unless we embedded a pointer to point to the row that contains the customer for each order. We could do this by creating an "owner" reference inside each order row that would contain the OID of the customer who placed the order.

A 19th-century philosophy professor named Augustus De Morgan penned an interesting poem to demonstrate this fundamental truth:

> *Great fleas have little fleas*
> *upon their backs to bite 'em*
> *And little fleas have lesser fleas,*
> *and so ad-infinitum.*
>
> *The great fleas themselves in turn*
> *has greater fleas to go on,*
> *while these again have greater still*
> *and greater still,*
> *and so on.*

Now, let's take a look how this type of recursive data relationship might be represented in an object/relational database such as Oracle8:

```
CREATE  TYPE  order_set
   AS  TABLE  OF  order;

CREATE  TABLE  CUSTOMER  (
   customer_id            integer,
   customer_full_name     full_name,
   customer_full_address  customer_address,
   .  .  .
   order_list             order_set);
```

Here we have nested the order table within the customer table! So, where do we go from here? How do we populate this new structure? Let's take a look at how this table might be populated:

```
INSERT INTO customer VALUES (
full_name ('ANDREW','S.','BURLESON),
customer_address('246 1st st.','Minot, ND','74635');
```

Now, we could add three orders for this customer;

```
INSERT INTO ORDER values order_id, customer_id,
    order_date (
9961
123,
SYSDATE);

INSERT INTO ORDER values order_id, customer_id,
    order_date (
9962
123,
SYSDATE);

INSERT INTO ORDER values order_id, customer_id,
    order_date (
9962
123,
SYSDATE);
```

Now, here comes the best part. We can now "pre-join" the customer table with the order table to add the three orders for this customer

```
UPDATE customer
  SET order_list (
    select REF(order) /* OID reference */
    from order
    WHERE
    order_date = SYSDATE
    and
    order.customer_ID = (123)
  )
```

So, what have we got here? It appears that the order_list entry in the customer table will contain "pointers" to the three orders that have been placed by this customer. As such, we are able to reference these pointers without having to perform a relational join.

```
SELECT DEREF(order_list)
from CUSTOMER
where
customer_id = 123; /* this will return 3 rows in
    the order table */
```

This query will return a pointer to the three rows in the order table. It should then be a simple matter to "de-reference" these pointers to retrieve the contents of the order table. Depending on the vendor implementation of the SQL, it might look something like this:

```
SELECT DEREF(order_list)
FROM customer
where customer_ID = 123;
```

Pointers to Whole Tables

The new object/relational database contains a very interesting pointer structure that allows a single cell in an entity to contain a whole other entity. In this way, it is possible to create a structure where objects (or tables) may be nested within other objects (or tables). For an object/relational database, this means that a single columns values in a table may contain a whole table. These sub-table tables, in turn, may have single column values that point to whole tables, and so on, ad infinitum (Figure 6.4).

While the application of this new data structure is not apparent, it does present exciting possibilities for modeling complex aggregate objects. In a C++ object-oriented databases such as Ontos or Objectivity, we can create a structure where an object contains a list of pointers. Each of these pointers, in turn will point to a separate list of pointers. These pointers will point to other objects in the database. In C language parlance, this structure is known as **char (pronounced star star char), which is called a pointer to a pointer to a character.

In object/relational databases, this structure is implemented by using what is called a "store table." The top-level table will contain a cell that is defined as a pointer to a table. The column that is defined as a pointer to a whole table has one big restriction in that each and every pointer must point to a table with the exact same definition. That is, each column value must contain a pointer to a table that is defined with the exact same definition.

While it appears that each cell points to a whole table, object/relational databases implement this structure by defining a store table. A store table is an internal table that is tightly coupled with the owner table, and the store

Employee table

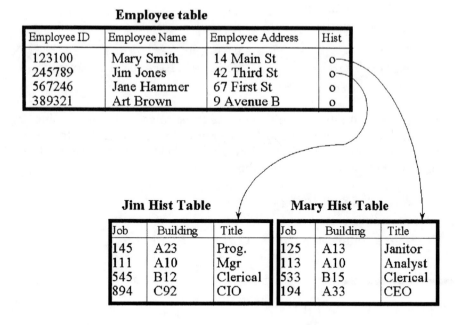

Employee ID	Employee Name	Employee Address	Hist
123100	Mary Smith	14 Main St	o—
245789	Jim Jones	42 Third St	o—
567246	Jane Hammer	67 First St	o
389321	Art Brown	9 Avenue B	o

Jim Hist Table

Job	Building	Title
145	A23	Prog.
111	A10	Mgr
545	B12	Clerical
894	C92	CIO

Mary Hist Table

Job	Building	Title
125	A13	Janitor
113	A10	Analyst
533	B15	Clerical
194	A33	CEO

Figure 6.4 Nesting tables within tables.

table inherits the data storage characteristics of the parent table. These inherited characteristics include the initial extent for the table and the size of new extents.

In essence, a store table is nothing more than an internal table that is defined as subordinate to the owner table with a fixed set of columns. Let's illustrate the use of this data structure with a simple example. Suppose that we start with a university database that has a many-to-many relationship between courses and student entities; that is, a student may take many courses, and a course has many students. In a traditional relational system, this relationship between students and courses would be implemented by creating a junction table between the student and course entities, and copying the primary keys from the student and course tables into this entity. In our example, this entity is called grade, and the grade entity contains the student_ID and the course_ID columns as foreign keys (Figure 6.5).

Now let's take a look at how this would be implemented using pointers to whole tables. To produce a class schedule for a student in a traditional relational implementation, we would need to select the student row, and then join with the grade table, and finally join with the class table:

```
SELECT
     student_full_name,
     course_name,
```

```
    course_date,
    grade
FROM
    student, grade, course
WHERE
    student_last_name = 'Burleson'
    AND
    student.student_ID = grade.student_ID
    AND
    grade.course_ID = course.course_ID;
```

To avoid the three-way SQL join of the tables, we could choose to create a store table that is subordinate to the student table. This table would contain the course_name, the course_date and the grade for each student.

```
CREATE TYPE
    student_list (
    student_full_name    full_name,
    student_full_address full_address,
    grade char(1));
```

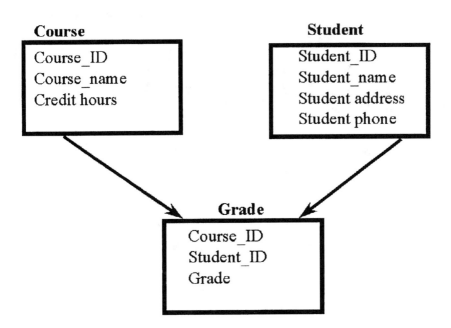

Figure 6.5 A sample many-to-many data relationship for a university.

```
CREATE TYPE student_list_type AS TABLE OF
    student_list;

CREATE TABLE
  COURSE (
     course_name      varchar(20),
     dept_ID          number(4),
     credit_hrs       number(2),
     student_roster   student_list_type);
```

Here we see that the student_roster column of the COURSE table contains a pointer to a table of type student_list. Herein lies the illusion. While it may appear to the application that each distinct column value points to a whole table, in reality the column points to a set or rows within the store table. The store table is common to all of the columns that contain this pointer structure, and the store table contains a special OID that points to the "owner" of the row in the parent table (Figure 6.6).

While the idea of nesting tables within tables is an excellent method for modeling hierarchical structures, there is still some question about the application of this data structure to real-world data models. The one nice feature

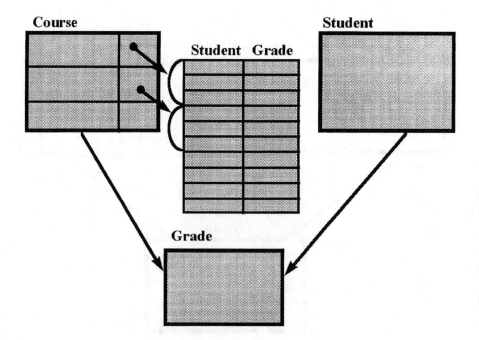

Figure 6.6 The physical implementation of a store table.

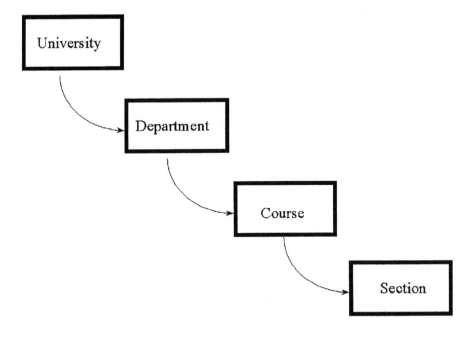

Figure 6.7 A natural hierarchy of data relationships

of nested tables is that a single select statement will return all of the applicable rows in the store table, thereby simplifying the query. Since the nested table is really just another table with the same column structure for each row, there is still some question about whether it is better to use this structure or to simply create another table.

Multidimensional Pointers

To understand multidimensional pointers, begin with a simple example of a natural hierarchy (Figure 6.7). In this example, we see that each university has many departments, each department offers many courses, and that each course offers many sections. This is a natural descending hierarchy of one-to-many relationships.

Let's take a look at how we could create a data structure that would embed pointers to establish these relationships.

Department table

```
department_name
(1-20)  *course
```

Course table

```
course number
course_name
(0-10) *section
(1) *department
```

Section table

```
section_number
semester
instructor_name
building
room
days
time
(1) *course
```

From this definition, we see that the department table consists of the department name, followed by from one to 20 pointers to courses. The course table contains the course number and course name followed by from zero to ten pointers to sections and one "owner" pointer, pointing to the departments row. The section table consists mostly of data items, except for the pointer to the course row.

We know there are many options for modeling this type of descending one-to-many data relationship. In a "vanilla" relational database, each entity would exist as a table, with the primary key of the owner table copied into the member table. But there is an alternative to modeling this structure in the object/relational model. Let's take a look at how a hierarchical data structure might be implemented in Oracle8:

```
CREATE TYPE full_name (
    first_name        varchar(20),
    MI                char(1),
    last_name         varchar(20));

CREATE TYPE section_type (
    section_number    number(5),
    instructor_name   full_name,
    semester          char(3),
    building          varchar(20),
```

```
    room                char(4),
    days_met            char(5),
    time_met            char(20));

CREATE TABLE section OF section_type;

CREATE TYPE section_array AS VARRAY(10) OF
      section_type;

CREATE TYPE course_type (
    course_ID           number(5),
    course_name         varchar(20),
    credit_hours        number(2),
    section_list        section_array);

CREATE TABLE course OF course_type;

CREATE TYPE course_array as VARRAY(20) OF
      course_type;

CREATE TYPE dept_type (
    dept_name           varchar(20),
    chairperson_name    full_name,
    course_list         course_array);

CREATE TABLE department OF dept_type;
```

This data structure is shown in Figure 6.8. We see that the pointers allow fast access from owner to member in the hierarchy, but where are the "owner" pointers? As it turns out, we must first define the hierarchy before we have the necessary definitions to include the pointers. Let's add them using the ALTER TYPE statement:

ALTER TYPE section_type
    ADD COLUMN course_owner_pointer course_type;

ALTER TYPE course_type
    ADD COLUMN department_owner_pointer department_type;

We have now created a two-way pointer structure, such that all owner rows in the hierarchy point to their member rows, while all member rows will point up to their owners. However, we must bear in mind that these are only

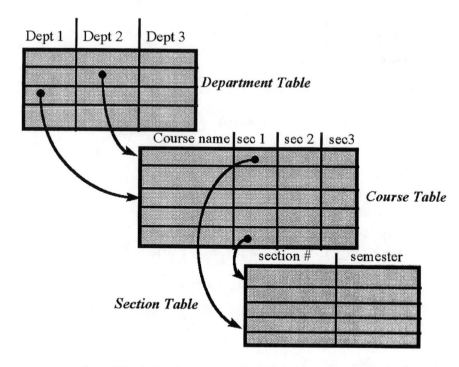

Figure 6.8 An implementation of multidimensional row pointers

data structures; it is up to the programmer, to assign these pointers when the rows are created.

In a sense, this data structure is the object/relational equivalent to the **char data structure. Essentially, a **char data structure is a structure where we have a pointer to an array of pointers to characters. In Oracle, the department has an array of pointers to courses, which, in turn, contain arrays of pointers to sections.

But how do we query these pointers with SQL? In order to accommodate the new object features, most object/relational vendors are implementing the CAST and the MULTISET extensions to SQL. For example, here is what the query to populate the student_list internal table:

```
INSERT INTO
  COURSE (STUDENT_LIST)
  (CAST
    (MULTISET
      (SELECT
        student_name,
        student_address,
        grade
```

```
     FROM
       GRADE,  STUDENT
     WHERE
       GRADE.course_name  =   CS101
       AND
       GRADE.student_name = STUDENT.student_name
    )
   )
 );
```

As we can see, the new SQL extensions are rather foreign to those who are accustomed to pure relational syntax.

Implications of Pointers for Database Design

So, we can now see that the ability to support abstract data types provides us with a lot of very powerful features, including:

1. The ability to store repeating groups within a cell of a table.
2. The ability to "nest" tables within tables.
3. The ability to provide pointer-based navigation for relational data.
4. The ability to represent aggregate objects.

Consider the ramifications for item pointer-based navigation to relational data. If we are allowed to bypass SQL, imagine the possibilities! With Oracle8 we could navigate a data model without having the overhead of joining tables together. More importantly, we now have the ability to represent "complex" objects. This means that we can precreate objects that are composed of subobjects without having to build them each time that we want to see them. Since the aggregate objects have an independent existence, we can attach methods to these objects. In addition, we can also save database overhead by precreating complex database objects, having them instantly available to the database. To illustrate this concept, let's create an order_form for a customer. When a customer places an order, she telephones the order department and indicates the following:

Her name, address, and payment method.
Her choices of items and the quantities for each item.

In a traditional relational database we would populate three tables to represent this relationship. They would be the CUSTOMER, ORDER, ORDER_LINE, and ITEM tables. Creating the order form would involve the following SQL:

```
SELECT
    customer.first_name,
    customer.last_name,
    customer.street_address,
    customer.city_address,
    customer.zip_code,
    customer.payment_method,
    order.order_date,
    item.item_description,
    order_line.quantity_ordered,
    item.item_price,
    order_line.quantity_ordered * item.item_price
FROM
    customer,
    order,
    order_line,
    item
WHERE
    order.customer_ID = customer.customer_ID
AND
    order.order_ID = order_line.order_ID
AND
    order_line.item_ID = item.item_ID
AND
    customer.customer_ID = 123;
```

As we can clearly see, the recreation of the data for an order form would involve a four-way table join. Using the object-relational features of abstract data types ADTs, we could define a new object called order_form that would contain all of the pointers to the various components that comprise the order form. Note that it is never necessary to re-build an order_form object unless items are deleted or added to the order_form. For example, when the quantity_ordered column in the order_line table is changed, the order_form object will automatically pick-up this new value when the order_line row is dereferenced.

Here's how it might work. We first need to define a pointer to return the row that corresponds to the customer who has placed the order. Let's assume that we have already created an ADT for the entire customer row and defined the customer table as follows:

```
CREATE TABLE customer (customer_data customer_adt);
```

We can now create a customer_ref type to hold the pointer to the customer:

```
CREATE TYPE customer_ref
AS TABLE OF customer_adt;
```

Since we will only be retrieving one order row, we can do the same thing for the order table row.

```
CREATE TYPE order_ref
AS TABLE OF order_adt;
```

Therefore, the first component of the order_form object will be the reference to the customer and order rows:

```
CREATE TABLE order_form (
  customer  customer_ref,
  order     order_ref);
```

Now that we have the customer and order data, we need to establish the pointers to represent the many-to-many relationship between the ORDER and the ITEM tables. Let's start by defining a repeating group of all of the order_lines for each order:

```
CREATE TYPE item_list
AS TABLE OF order_line;
```

Now, that we have defined the item_list, let's take a stab at defining a order_form:

```
CREATE TABLE order_form (
  customer  customer_ref,
  order     order_ref,
  lines     item_list);
```

Now, we will need to establish pointers to all of the items that are referenced in the order_line table. But how can we do this? We do not know the item_ID numbers that participate in the order until we have retrieved the order_line rows. In this case we need to establish "owner" pointers inside each order_line row so that we will be able to de-reference the item table. Let's assume that the line_item table has been defined as shown below to include a reference pointer to the item table:

```
/* example of an owner pointer */
CREATE TYPE item_ref
  AS TABLE OF item;

CREATE TABLE line_item (
  order_ID        integer,
  item_ID         integer,
  item_pointer    item_ref,
  quantity_ordered integer);
```

So, let's see how we could display all of the data for the order_form object:

```
CREATE TABLE order_form (
  customer        customer_ref,
  order           order_ref,
  lines           item_list);

SELECT
  DEREF(customer.customer_last_name),
  DEREF . . .
  DEREF(order.order_date),
  DEREF(item_list.item_name), /* if item is a
      foreign key in line item */
  DEREF(order.quantity_ordered)
  DEREF(DEREF(order_line.item_pointer)) /* this
      returns item data */
```

Pointer Twizzling

The concept of storing a pointer to an array of pointers (**char in C++) has another remarkable feature. Since we have a pseudo-table with all of the pointers for rows in a table, we can change the sequence of these row references without ever accessing the rows themselves. In object-oriented parlance this concept is known as pointer "twizzling."

Note: A row can only be referenced if it has been defined with an OID. To do this the table must be defined as:

```
CREATE TABLE customer OF customer_stuff;
```

as opposed to:

```
CREATE TABLE customer
(
customer_data customer_stuff
);
```

These are the SAME table definitions; the only difference is that the first has a column called OID$ that contains a unique object-ID for each row.

Aggregate Objects and Pointers

Aggregrate diagrams are used to describe objects that are composed of smaller objects within the database. For example, we may have an order form that is composed entirely of pointers to other entities. Here is the description of the order_form.

```
order_form
agg-table
customer_data
order_data
item_list(10)
total
```

Note the implied relationships to other objects. Because the order_form does not contain any of its own data, we see that it is similar to a relational "view." However, there is one important exception. While a view serves to consolidate data from many base tables, it is always created at runtime. Unlike views, aggregate objects are prebuilt, and have their own independent existence. In the above example, we have prebuilt all of the order forms, and we have presorted all of the order information, placing each item in the proper order. Since all of the items are presorted, we do not have to do any run-time sorting of rows to get the requested information in the proper order.

Since we are talking about pointers to objects, we need to come up with a convention for noting pointers to rows. In an object database, pointers are not generic. Object databases use a principle called strong typing which means that a pointer that has been defined as a pointer to an order object will not be able to accept a pointer to any other object.

In the C language, pointers are described with an asterisk. For example, pointers to orders would be described as *order and pointers to a customer object would be described as *customer.

We will use this notation to describe aggregate objects. With an objects data structure, we may see a single pointer to another object or a series of pointers to other objects. As such, we will denote a series of pointers within parenthesis, showing the lower and upper bounds of the pointers. For example, consider the following pointer list definitions:

```
(0-3)  *Job_history
(1-4)  *items
```

Here we see that the first item is an array of pointers that may contain from zero to three pointers to job_history objects. The second line shows a pointer array with from one to four pointers to item objects.

Now, let's take a look at what an order_form object might look like:

```
order_form
(1)    *customer
(1)    *order
(1-10) *item
(1-10) *quantity_ordered
order_total_amount
```

Here we see that an order_form consists of one pointer to a customer object, one pointer to an order object, from one through 10 pointers to item objects, and from one through ten pointers to quantity_ordered objects. When a pre-assembled order_form is accessed, the database will de-reference these pointers and display the data within the target object or row, within an object/relational database.

Since many aggregate objects consists almost entirely of pointers, it is very tempting to include an order_form entity on the E/R model with a box for the order_form entity, and sets into every base object in the model.

Note that we have deliberately introduced order_total_amount as the only data item in the order form object. While this number could be re-computed each time that a data item is displayed, we can choose to introduce the order total as a form of planned redundancy, knowing that this values would need to be re-computed whenever any of the order information has changed.

As we can see there can be so many aggregate entities that it is often too complex to include each and every aggregate object in the E/R model. Hence, to avoid a "plate of spaghetti" with hundreds of arrows, we include all of the aggregate objects on another diagram (Figure 6.9).

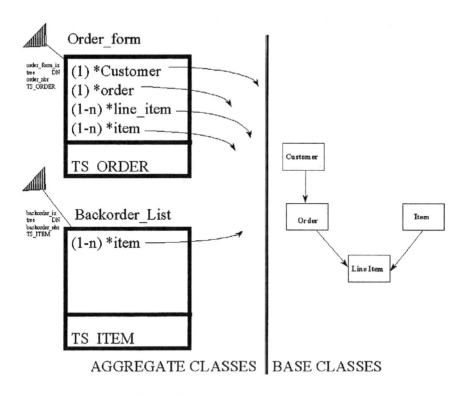

AGGREGATE CLASSES | BASE CLASSES

Figure 6.9 An aggregate class diagram.

Note that it is possible to have aggregate objects that are composed of other aggregate objects. For example, consider the relationship between a class roster and an instructor roster. As class_roster is an aggregate object consisting of pointers to one course object and many student objects. An instructor object is an object than contains a pointer to an instructor object, and many pointers to class_roster objects.

```
Class_roster (class_ID)
*student (student_name, student_ID)

Instructor_roster (instructor_ID)
(1-1) *instructor(instructor_name,
    instructor_address)
(1-n) *class_roster (class_name, student_name)
```

Here we see that a class roster has the class_ID for a primary key. Included in the class_roster object is a pointer to the pertinent instructor row (denoted by *instructor). The instructor roster has the class_roster embedded within the definition, and we see that the instructor_roster consists of one pointer to an instructor, and a pointer to the class_roster objects. Note that this is the equivalent of a C++ array of pointers (as denoted by **student).

Summary

Now that we have a basic understanding of how pointers are declared and implemented within the object/relational model, let's move on to take a look at some of the other constructs of the object/relational databases including class hierarchies and inheritance, and the use of methods.

7

Database Objects and Inheritance

Inheritance is a frequently misunderstood feature of object databases. Essentially, inheritance is defined as the ability of a lower-level object to inherit, or access, the data structures and behaviors associated with all classes which are above it in the class hierarchy.

One of the most common misunderstandings about inheritance has to do with the difference between a class hierarchy and the relationships between objects in the database. In the object/relational model, object relationships are established either by foreign keys or by OIDs, and these data relationships have absolutely nothing to do with inheritance. For example, it is a very common misconception that order objects "inherit" the data from the customer that placed the order (Figure 7.1).

It is critical to understand that inheritance only occurs twice in the life of a database object. At object creation time, the object is instantiated by gathering the data items from all classes in the hierarchy. To conceptualize the use of a class, think of a class as a "rubber stamp" that creates objects, using the data structures that have been specified in the class definition.

The only other time that inheritance takes place is when an object receives a message from an application program. This message invokes a "method," which is a behavior or code-snippet, that performs a specific operation on the object. The object first looks in its class definition for the method. If the method is not found, the database looks in all of the superclasses in the class hierarchy to find the method. This search process for methods is commonly known as "late binding," since the application does not bind with the method until the moment that it is called.

In an object/relational database such as Oracle8, late binding can cause significant stress on the library cache and slow down performance. As a consequence, late binding may be turned off, and the target class for a method may be directly specified. This makes the code run much faster since the database is not required to search the class hierarchy at runtime.

Methods with the same name may be placed at different levels in the class hierarchy whenever it is appropriate for a method to behave differently in different classes. Methods that are placed lower in the class hierarchy are said to be "overloaded" methods, in the sense that the lower-level objects will encounter these methods first and will not access the higher-level method with the same name.

131

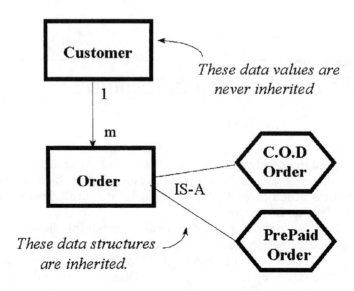

Figure 7.1   The difference between inheritance and data access.

Polymorphism and Inheritance

The idea of having methods with the same name is known in object parlance a "polymorphism." This is a Greek term, which literally translated means "many forms." For example, the process called compute_paycheck may be quite different for different classes of employees. An executive paycheck may include stock options and will not require a statement of the number of hours worked, while a blue-collar workers paycheck depends upon a wage grade and the number of hours that are worked. These are considered polymorphic because they both server to compute paychecks, but they perform the operation in vastly different ways. Fortunately, these complexities are hidden from the application, since the object database will recognize the type of object that is the target of the method, and invoke the appropriate method.

The Two Types of Polymorphism

There are two types of polymorphism in object/relational databases. In addition to the type of polymorphism that we just described, the object/relational databases allow for polymorphism to be implemented by using different input parameters to a method. For example, suppose that there are two functions with identical names, but one function accepts an integer while the other accepts a character string. In the basic language the "+" operator is polymorphic.

When the + operator is passed integers it adds the integers together.

```
newval = weight + cost;
```

However, when the + operator is surrounded by strings it knows to perform a concatenation operation:

```
full_name = first_name + last_name;
```

The "IS-A" Relationship and Inheritance

We must always remember that inheritance and class hierarchies apply only to database entities that are different types of the same thing. In Figure 7.2 we see a class hierarchy for the person type. As we see a person may be a customer, an employee, or a contractor. Further, an employee may be either an executive, salaried, or wage employee.

The class hierarchy diagram is used to describe all of the data structures and methods that can be inherited by a database object. In essence, a class

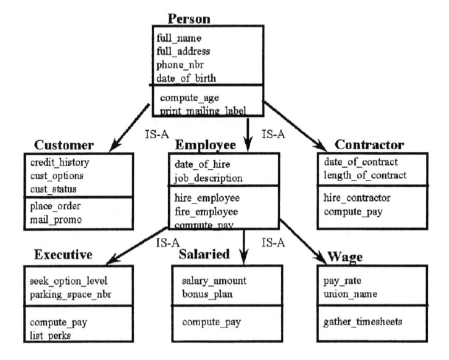

Figure 7.2 A sample class hierarchy for the person entity.

hierarchy diagram consists of two parts, and we notice that each class is divided into two halves, with the data attributes listed in the top half, and the methods listed in the bottom half. The details for each section include the following:

1. **Data Type List** — These are all of the data structures that are inherited by lower-level objects when they are instantiated. Note that some properties such as value constraints can also be inherited. For example, the vehicle_color data structure will also contain validation rules, to insure that the colors are either RED, BLUE, GREEN, or YELLOW. Here is a sample data structure for vehicle_color:

   vehicle_color varchar(15),

      CONSTRAINT valid_color

        vehicle_color in

      "RED," "BLUE," "GREEN," "YELLOW"

2. **Method List** — This section describes all of the methods associated with a class. The information here includes the method name, the required input parameters, and the return value. In the following example, the compute_charge method accepts the vehicle ID and the return data. The compute_charge method then performs the computation (the details of which are hidden from the application), and returns a number for the charge.

It is important to examine Figure 7.2 to understand inheritance. In the person class we see those data attributes that are common to all people including their name, address, phone number and date of birth. Moving down the class hierarchy, we see that different "types" of people have different data attributes that are unique to their class. For example, we see that the pay_rate data attribute appears only in the wage employee class, since this data attribute would be inappropriate for use in the executive or salaried employee class definition.

We also see that some method names are replicated. While the names are replicated, the internal process code for these methods may be very different. For example, the compute_pay methods appears in the contractor class as well as the employee class, since the process of computing pay is very different for these classes of people. Also, within the employee class, we see that compute_pay also appears in the executive and salaried classes. This process is called *overloading*. The wage class will inherit the compute_pay method from the employee class, but since the processes of computing pay is different for executives and salaried employees, the database designer has overloaded the compute_pay method, and created different methods with the same name in these sub-classes.

Remember, a class hierarchy is a *definition* of the objects, and serves as the rubber stamp that the object database uses when the object is created. As such, there are some class definition that exist solely for the purpose of passing data structures and methods to the lower level classes. In our example we see can infer that our database would never use the person class definition to create an object, but uses the person class as what is know in object parlance as the *base class*. A base class is never used to stamp out objects, but only serves to pass the data structures and methods to its sub-classes.

After establishing a class hierarchy with the entity/relationship model, the principle of generalization is used to identity the class hierarchy and the level of abstraction associated with each class (Figure 7.2). Generalization implies a successive refinement of the class, allowing the superclasses of objects to inherit the data attributes and behaviors that apply to the lower levels of the class. Generalization establishes taxonomy hierarchies, which organize the classes according to their characteristics, usually in increasing levels of detail. Generalization begins at a very general level, and proceeds to a specific level, with each sub-level having its own unique data attributes and behaviors.

It is not uncommon to see entity/relation models with numerous class hierarchies. In Figure 7.3, the IS–A relationship is used to create a hierarchy within the object class, and all of the lower-level classes inherit the behaviors. The IS–A relationship is used to model the hierarchy which is created as the class entity is decomposed into its logical sub-components. Employees may be WAGE, SALARIED, or EXECUTIVE and software may be CLIENT-SERVER or MAINFRAME, each with their own data items and behaviors.

Not all classes within a generalization hierarchy will have objects associated with them. The object-oriented paradigm allows for abstraction, which means that a class may exist only for the purpose of passing inherited data and behaviors. The classes VEHICLE and CAR would probably not have any concrete objects, while objects within the VAN class would inherit from the abstract VEHICLE and CAR classes. Multiple inheritance is also demonstrated by the AMPHIBIAN_CAR class. Any instances of this class inherit data and behaviors from both the CAR and the BOAT classes.

It is important to clearly understand that there is a very big difference between one-to-many relationships and IS–A relationships. The IS–A construct does not imply any type of recurring association, while the one-to-many and many-to-many relationships imply multiple occurrences of the subclasses. In the above example, this entire class hierarchy describes vehicles which are associated with the ITEM entity in the overall database, and class hierarchies DO NOT imply any data relationships between the classes. While one CUSTOMER may place many ORDERS, it is not true that one ORDER may have many COD-ORDERS.

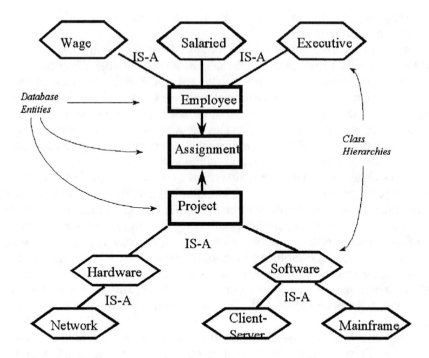

Figure 7.3   An entity/relation model for a project management system.

Multi-Level Inheritance Hierarchies

As we already know, inheritance is defined as the ability of a lower-level object to inherit or access the data structures and behaviors associated with all classes which are above it in the class hierarchy. Now, we will examine a more complex inheritance hierarchy (Figure 7.4). Here we examine an application of inheritance for a vehicle dealership. Occurrences of ITEMs to a dealership are VEHICLES; beneath the vehicle class, we may find subclasses for cars, boats, and for aircraft. Within cars, the classes may be further partitioned into classes for TRUCK and VAN, and SEDAN. The VEHICLE class would contain the data items which are unique to vehicles, including the vehicle ID and the year of manufacture. The CAR class, because it IS-A VEHICLE, would inherit the data items of the VEHICLE class. The CAR class might contain data items such as the number of axles and the gross weight of the vehicle. Because the VAN class IS-A CAR, which in turn IS-A VEHICLE, objects of the VAN class will inherit all data structures and behaviors relating to CARS and VEHICLES.

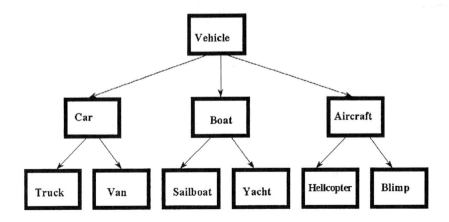

Figure 7.4 A sample class hierarchy for vehicles

Note: It is critical to the understanding of inheritance to note that inheritance happens at different times during the life of an object.

Inheritance of Data Structures

At object creation time, inheritance is the mechanism whereby the initial data structure for the object is created. It is critical to note that only data structures are inherited, never data. It is a common misconception that data is inherited, such that an order may inherit the data items for the customer that placed the order. We must understand that inheritance is only used to create the initial, empty data structures for the object. In our example, all vehicles would inherit data definitions in the VEHICLE class, while an object of a lower-level class (say, SAILBOAT) would inherit data structures that only apply to sailboats—as in sail_size.

Inheritance of Methods

Inheritance also happens at runtime when a call to a method (stored procedure) is made. For example, assume that the following call is made to sailboat object:

```
SAILBOAT.compute_rental_charges();
```

The database first searches for the compute_rental_charges in the sailboat class; if it is not found, the database searches up the class hierarchy until compute_rental_charges is located.

Inheritance in Action

Let us see how inheritance might work within a database object. As we recall, inheritance occurs at two times during the life of an object: when the object is created, data structures are inherited, and at runtime, methods may be inherited from the class hierarchy.

In a university database, we have several types of students. The main question when designing classes is to ask whether the different types of students will have different data or different behaviors. Your analysis of the data has derived the following data definitions for students:

```
CREATE CLASS student (
  student_ID                    number (5);
  student_name
    first_name                  varchar(20),
    MI                          char(1),
    last_name                   varchar(20)
  )

METHODS
  void enroll_student (student_struct *student),
  void graduate_student(student_struct *student);
  int compute_tuition(student_struct *student);

CREATE CLASS graduate_student
  WITHIN CLASS student
(
  undergraduate_degree        char(3)
    CONSTRAINT undergraduate_degree in ('BA','BS'),
  undergraduate_major         varchar(20,
  undergraduate_school_name   varchar(30);
  undergraduate_school_address
    street_address            varchar(20),
    city_name                 varchar(20),
    zip_code                  number(9),
  mentor_name                 varchar(20),
  thesis_review_date          date)
```

```
METHODS
    *professor assign_mentor(student_struct
         *student);

CREATE CLASS non_resident_student WITHIN CLASS
         student
    state_of_origin            char(2),
    region_of_origin           char(5)
      CONSTRAINT region_of_origin in ('NORTH',
         'SOUTH','EAST','WEST')

METHODS
    int compute_tuition(student_struct *student);

CREATE CLASS foreign_student WITHIN CLASS
         non_resident_student (
    country_of_origin          varchar(20),
    visa_expiration_date       date)

METHODS
    validate_visa_status(student_struct *student);
```

Note: This university does not allow foreign or non-resident students into its graduate school, and this is why we see that the graduate_school is only a subclass of the student class.

You also may note the references to pointers in the code snippet. For example, consider the following method definition:

```
*professor assign_mentor(student_struct
     *student);
```

This statement is saying that the method called assign_mentor accepts an input variable called student_struct which is of the data type "pointer to student" (*student). The assign_mentor methods returns a pointer to a professor (*professor). Remember, in the object/relational model we can capitalize on the use of these pointers, and it is far easier to pass a pointer that to pass the entire data structure. In the case of the assign_mentor method, the pointer called student_struct will be "de-referenced", and the method will have access to the student data. Methods are described in more detail in the next chapter.

Now let's examine how these data structures will be used by the database at object creation time. When a foreign_student object is created, a data structure will be created that contains all of the data structures from each higher level object. For example, this is what the data structure would look like for a foreign_student:

```
student_ID              umber (5),

student_name
   first_name           varchar(20),
   MI                   char(1),
   last_name            varchar(20),

state_of_origin         char(2),

region_of_origin        char(5)
   CONSTRAINT region_of_origin in
   ('NORTH','SOUTH','EAST','WEST'),

country_of_origin       varchar(20),

visa_expiration_date    date);
```

Here we can see that a foreign_student would inherit the data structures contained in both the student as well as the non_resident_student classes in addition to it's own class data structures (Figure 7.5). When a foreign_student is created, it is treated as a student object, but the database is aware that it is a foreign_student and will always check the foreign_student object first before looking inside other student class definitions.

Also note that the constraint for valid values is also inherited into the data definition. Whenever a foreign_student object is created, the region_of_origin column must have one of the specified values.

Now let's examine the inheritance of the methods that we defined for these objects. When we invoke the compute_tuition method for a non-resident student we see that this method exists within the non_resident class definition. This indicates that there must be some different process for computing tuition for non_resident students. Essentially, we have "overloaded" the compute_tuition process in the student class, and the new method is said to be "polymorphic," in that it servers to compute tuition just like the method in the student class, but it does this function in a very different way.

When we invoke the compute_tuition method for a foreign_student, we note that this method has not been defined within the foreign_student class. Hence, the object database will retrieve and execute the compute_tuition method from the student class.

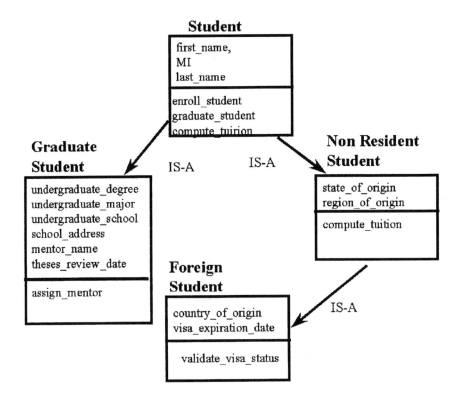

Figure 7.5 The student class hierarchy.

As we mentioned earlier, this is called "late-binding" and can cause performance problems within object/relational databases. Most object/relational databases allow for late binding to be turned off (on a class by class basis), by directing the class method definition to go directly to the student class to find the method. But beware, late-binding can be a very powerful feature and should not be turned off indiscriminately. Without late-binding, it is impossible to overload a method.

Overloading a Class Definition

Remember, overloading is a very powerful feature whereby a process can be slightly altered by creating a different version of the method and attaching the new method further down in the class hierarchy (Figure 7.6). When this is done, only objects of that data class will have access to the modified method, and the developer can be absolutely certain that there will be no unintended side-effects from their code change.

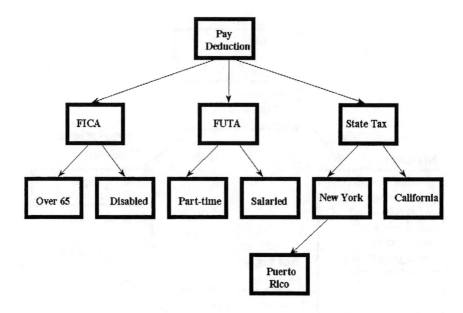

Figure 7.6 An example of method overloading.

In Figure 7.6, we see that the State tax deductions for Puerto Rico are almost identical to those of New York, with some very small changes. We can then create a new subclass to the New York class called Puerto Rico, and overload only those New York methods that are different. All of the identical methods will be inherited by the Puerto Rico class from the New York superclass.

Now that we understand the basic concepts of inheritance, lets take a look at a special case of inheritance called "multiple inheritance."

Multiple Inheritance

To further confuse matters, the term "multiple inheritance" refers to the ability of an object to inherit attributes and behaviors from more than one superclass. This ability is especially useful for "junction" objects which inherit from more than one superclass. For example, a Seaplane may inherit data structures and methods from both the Airplane and the Boat superclasses (Figure 7.7).

Multiple inheritance can lead to serious problems. When an object is created, it is possible that the inherited data structures may contain identical data structures, and the object will not be able to resolve the duplicate data names. At runtime, multiple inheritance can lead to a conflict as the database must search up two paths when looking for a method. If two methods are

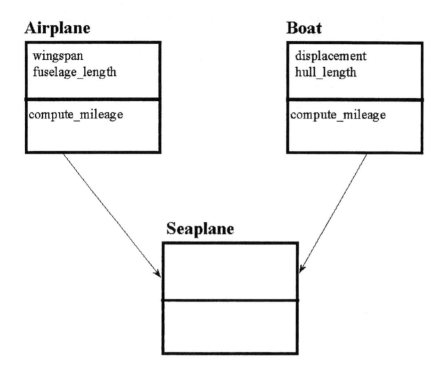

Figure 7.7   An example of multiple inheritance

found within each tree, the databases will become confused about which method to execute. For example, the method compute_mileage could be invoked for the Seaplane object. In the Airplane, we may have a compute_mileage method that computers mileage in statute miles, while at the same time, the Boat superclass may contain a compute_mileage method that computes mileage in nautical miles. Fortunately multiple inheritance is rarely needed in the database object model and is usually not supported by the vendors.

Summary

We should now have an understanding of the basic concepts of inheritance and how it is used within database objects. Reviewing the basic tenets of database object inheritance:

1. Inheritance only occurs at object creation time and when a method is invoked.

2. At object creation time, only data definitions are inherited. Data values are never inherited. They must be accessed.

3. At runtime, inheritance is used to locate the desired method.

Now that we understand the basic dynamics of class hierarchies and inheritance, let's see how we can use these methods to derive a hierarchy of system behaviors that allows for flexibility in our application design.

8

Methods and Database Objects

If we review the evolution of databases from the earliest hierarchical systems to today's object-oriented databases, the single most important new feature is the coupling of data with the behavior of data. While the flat-file systems brought us data storage, the hierarchical and the network databases added the ability to create relationships between data, the relational database brought declarative data query: we now see the coupling of the data with the behavior of the data. For the purposes of this book, we will use the terms behavior, process code, and method interchangeably, since different vendor implementations use these synonymous terms to describe embedded process code.

One of the huge benefits of the object-relational architecture is the ability to move procedures out of application programs and into the database engine. In addition to providing a more secure repository for the code, the ability to tie data and behavior together also enhances the ability to reuse routines. When combined with the ability to directly represent aggregate objects, we now have a framework for coupling all data processes directly with the object that contains the data that will be manipulated.

While this may seem like a trivial feature at first glance, it holds tremendous ramifications for systems development. Since the process code now moves into the database along with the data, the job of database administrators (DBAs) and system developers will change radically. The DBA, whose exclusive domain was the proprietorship of the data, must now take on additional responsibility for management of the behaviors that are stored in the database. Programmers will no longer have the freedom to write custom-crafted code anytime they wish. With the introduction of reusable methods, the programmer changes from a custom craftsman to a code assembler, very much like the jobs of craftsmen changed with the introduction of mass production in the industrial revolution of the late eighteenth century.

But why were methods introduced into the database object model? Some of the most commonly cited reasons include:

1. **Code Reusability** — Process code only needs to be written once, and the fully tested and reliable process code can then be included in many different applications.

2. **Control Over the Environment** — By making the database a central repository for process code, all of the processes are stored in a common format and in a central location. The benefits from this approach include the ability to quickly find code, as well as the ability to scan the process code with text-search ability.

3. **Proactive Tuning** — Since all of the SQL is present in the database, the DBA can extract and test the access methods used by all SQL for the application. This information can be used to identify indexes that need to be created, tables that may benefit from caching in the buffer pool, and other DBA tuning techniques. In addition, the developers can use this central repository to tune their SQL, adding hints and changing the SQL in order to obtain an optimal access path to the data.

4. **Application Portability** — Since all of the application code resides in a platform independent language within the database, the application consists exclusively of calls to the methods that invoke the processes. As such, an application front-end can easily be ported from one platform to another without any fear that the process code will need to change.

5. **Cross-Referencing of Processes** — Since the data dictionary for the database will keep track of all of the programs that call the data, it is very easy to keep track of where a method is used, and what methods are nested within other methods. This feature greatly simplifies systems maintenance, since all applications that reference a particular entity can be easily and reliably identified.

Another nice feature of the coupling of data and behavior is the elimination of the "code hunt" and the subsequent code reusability that will result. In order to meet the promise of code reusability for database objects, the programmer must first know where to find the method. By using a methods browser, the programmer could quickly scan the methods attached to each database object, and hopefully find the proper method, thereby alleviating the need to rewrite the code.

Planning the Method Hierarchy

While the coupling of data with behaviors is a revolutionary concept for database management, the failure to properly plan the implementation can be a disaster. In order to achieve the benefits of using methods, a careful decomposition of the processes must take place. As we discussed, there are three types of processes, those that are independent of the database classes,

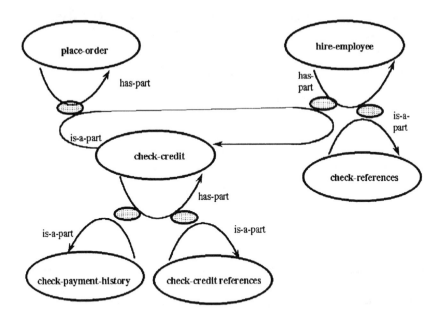

Figure 8.1 The recursive many-to-many nature of method nesting.

those that are attached to a base-level database class, and those that are attached to aggregate database classes. In addition, any method may have other methods nested within its structure, while at the same time participating as a submethod within another method (Figure 8.1).

Here we see that the check_credit() method is composed of the sub-processes, check_payment_history() and check_credit_references() methods. At the same time, check_credit() participates in the place_order() and the hire_employee() methods. Given this huge array of choices, where do we begin developing the methods? There is a sequence of events that must take place to achieve this mapping of methods to classes:

1. Before the mapping of methods to classes can begin, you should have already created the following analysis and design documents:

    • A set of fully decomposed data-flow diagrams for your system. This will be used as the specification for all of the methods. From the DFD we will gather the method names, the input and output values, and the breakdown of nested methods.

    • A entity/relationship diagram for the system. This diagram will be used to identify the base classes for the system.

    • An aggregate object diagram. This diagram is used to associate the higher level processes with the methods that will be attached to these classes.

2. From the DFD, create a prototype for every process on the data flow diagram. This will formally state the input and output parameters for each process on all levels of the DFD.

3. Identify and prototype all standalone functions in the system.

4. Map the prototypes to the entities.

While this mapping of processes to methods may seem to be a straightforward approach, there are many new concepts that a traditional analyst my not be familiar with using. For the purpose of illustration, we will use the running example from our order processing system that was discussed in earlier chapters and use as our mapping example the sub-processes that are contained within the fill_order process.

The Functional Specifications (Data-Flow Diagrams)

The generally accepted starting point is with either a traditional data-flow diagram or a functional model. (Recall from Chapter 3 that a data-flow diagram and functional model are almost the same thing.) Let's begin by doing a short review of object analysis. A functional specification for any system describes the complete logical model and consists of three documents. The data-flow diagram is a pictorial description of all of the processes in the system, and it is supplemented with two other documents. The data dictionary, that is used to define all of the data flows and data stores in our system, and the process logic specifications (mini-specs) that are used to describe each process, showing how the data flow is modified within each process.

As discussed in Chapter 3 and our discussion of basic object analysis, we know that the data flow diagram is the foundation of any systems analysis. The DFD diagrams the processes, data flows and data stores as we decompose the system. While these documents may be known by different names depending upon the analysis methodology that is chosen, they should contain a complete description of all of the entities in our system. Let's begin by taking a level one data-flow diagram and showing the breakdown of the processes (Figure 8.2).

Here we see the overall specification for the "fill order" process, and we can easily see all of the incoming and outgoing data items. In this case, we see "cust_info" coming in as the input to the "fill order" process. Of course, "cust_info" does not tells us about the details of this data flow, and we must go to the data dictionary to see the contents of cust_info:

```
cust_info =

cust_full_name +
    cust_last_name
    cust_first_name
    cust_middle_initial

cust_full_address +
    cust_street_address
    cust_city_name
    cust_state
    cust_zip_code

cust_phone_nbr +

1
{ item_ID + item_quantity }
n
```

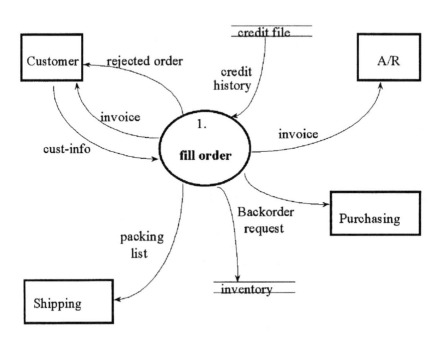

Figure 8.2 A Level One data-flow diagram for filling orders.

We will use these data dictionary definitions to gather the data items that are of interest to each process in our data flow diagram. Remember, the purpose of designing methods is to map the incoming and outgoing data flows to clean, well-defined procedures that can be coupled with the database entities.

Now let's take a look at how the fill_order process is decomposed into lower level DFDs. Looking at the next lowest level DFD (Figure 8.3), we see that fill_order is broken down into three sub-processes, check_customer_credit, check_inventory, and prepare_invoice. This DFD-shows all of the input and output data flows for these processes.

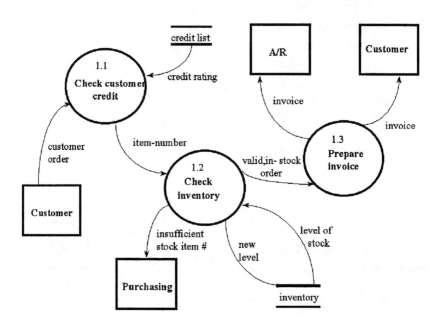

Figure 8.3   A Level Two data-flow diagram for the fill order process.

Here we see another level of detail for the fill_order process. This process is broken down into three sub-processes, each with its own data flows and processes. As we might guess, the departitioning of the processes will correspond to the departitioning of the methods for our object database.

Let's complete the foundation for our methods by showing the next level DFD for some of the lower-level processes, we will use the check_inventory process (Figure 8.4) and the prepare_invoice process (Figure 8.5). We can assume that these are 'functional primitive' processes, and they will serve as our lowest level methods in our example.

It is important for the mapping of methods to database objects to understand when a process has been departitioned to a level that corresponds with the functions of a database entity. We could continue to departition this DFD, making each process smaller and smaller, but the subprocesses would not easily map to the database objects. Hence, when we see that a process on our

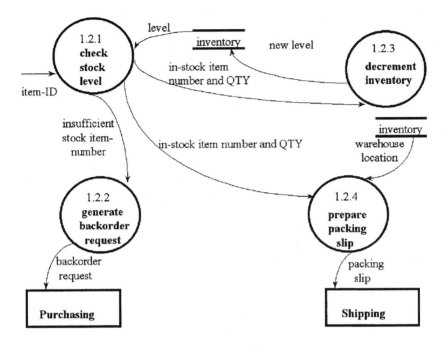

Figure 8.4 The data-flow diagram for the check_inventory process.

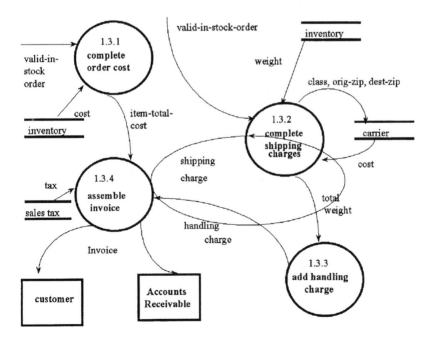

Figure 8.5 The data flow diagram for the prepare_invoice process.

DFD deals with a single function on a single database entity, we know that we have reached the 'functional primitive' level, and the analysis is complete.

Now that we have completed the functional specifications for this system we are ready to take these definitions and create the "prototypes" for the methods that will eventually become the methods for our database objects.

Creating the Method Prototypes

For the purposes of this example, we will take the data type definitions from the data dictionary and the psuedocode from the mini-spec to complete our understanding of the hierarchical mapping of methods. If we have performed our analysis properly, we will reference our set of data flow diagrams, beginning at level one (describing our fill_order process), and including all of the lower-level data flow diagrams.

Here we can begin by listing each process, and showing the sub-methods within each process:

```
1 - fill_order

    1.1 - check_customer_credit

    1.2 - check_inventory
            1.2.1 - check_stock_level
            1.2.2 - generate_backorder_notice
            1.2.3 - decrement_inventory
            1.2.4 - prepare_packing_slip

    1.3 - prepare_invoice
            1.3.1 - compute_order_cost
            1.3.2 - compute_shipping_charges
            1.3.3 - add_handling_charge
            1.3.4 - assemble_invoice
```

We should now be able to see how all of the methods are nested within other methods. Once this natural hierarchy has been developed we are ready to define the mapping of these processes to our database classes.

As we know, the lowest level data flow diagrams represent "functional primitives," or processes that cannot be decomposed into smaller processes. Of course, the functional primitive processes will become methods, but does this mean that they will never have subcomponents? If the analyst has performed their job properly there will be no submethods in these processes with the exception of standalone methods, such as a compute_shipping_charge method.

Beginning with the these primitive processes, we design a method that accepts the same values as noted on the DFD, and returns the same values to the program that invokes the method. For example, in Figure 8.5 we see that the complete-shipping-charges process accepts a valid-in-stock-order as input. Inside this process, it gathers the weight and cost of the items, computes the charges, and returns the shipping charge and total-weight.

Essentially, a prototype is a formal definition of a method that describes all of the input and output data flows. The accepted form for a prototype is:

```
return_data_type  Method_name
(input_data_name_1   input_data_type_1,
 input_data_name_2   input_data_type_2,
 . . .);
```

Before going into more detail, let's review the possible data types that are used by methods. These data types may be used to return a data value or they may be accepted by the method as an input parameter.

```
int — an integer value
varchar — a variable length character string
*type — a pointer to a data structure
```

The *type (pronounced star type) is the most confusing data type for most object novices since it refers to pointers. A pointer in an object database is an object identifier (OID) that points to the object that will supply the values to the method. Because most object-oriented databases support "strong data typing", we must differentiate between the different types of OIDs. For example, a pointer to an order (*order), is quite different from a pointer to a customer (*customer) object. As a practical matter it is more efficient to pass a pointer to the data than it is to pass the data itself, since the pointer (OID) is more compact.

In object database parlance, we design the "prototype" for each process on our DFDs. For example, let's begin by examining how we design the prototype for the compute_shipping_charge() method.

From our DFD, we see that compute_shipping_charges accepts a valid_in_stock_order, and outputs the shipping_charge for the order. Therefore, we could create a prototype that shows compute_shipping charges as returning an integer (the shipping charge), and accepting a pointer to an order object.

```
int compute_shipping_charge(valid_in_stock_order *order);
```

Returning to our data dictionary (not shown) we could see that valid_in_ stock_order contains four values that are required for this process to compute the shipping charges:

1. The objects weight in pounds.
2. The desired class of shipping.
3. The origination zip code.
4. The destination zip code.

So, how do we get these items, when we are only giver a pointer to an order? The method will de-reference the pointer to the order object and gather the required information. This means that the method will grab the OID and issue the appropriate SQL to accept all of the data items from the object. Here is what the SQL within the compute_shipping_charges method might look like:

```
SELECT
    item_weight,
    shipping_class,
    origination_zip_code,
    destination_zip_code
FROM
    ORDER
WHERE
    ORDER.OID = :valid_in_stock_order;
```

This function returns the shipping charge, expressed as an integer number.
If we did not pass the pointer to the order object to this method, the prototype for compute_shipping charges becomes far more complicated:

```
int compute_shipping_charge
    (weight int, class char(1),
    origination_zip_code number(9),
    destination_zip_code number(9));
```

Note that the first token "int" refers to the data type of the value that is returned by the method. For methods that do not return a value the first token in the prototype is "void". For example, a method called give_raise would not return a value, and could be prototyped as:

```
void give_raise(emp_ID number(9), percentage int);
```

Now that we understand the basics of prototyping, let's prototype every method from our example data flow diagrams.

```
*order      fill_order(cust_info *customer);
int         check_customer_credit(cust_info *customer);
int         check_inventory(item_number int);

*invoice    prepare_invoice(valid_in_stock_order
                 *order_form);
int         check_stock_level(item_number int);

*backorder  generate_backorder_request(item_number int);
void        decrement_inventory(item_number int);

*packing_slip prepare_packing_slip(valid_in_stock_order
                 *order_form);
int         compute_order_cost(valid_in_stock_order
                 *order_form);
int         compute_shipping_charges(valid_in_stock_order
                 *order_form);
int         add_handling_charge(total_weight int);

*invoice    assemble_invoice(item_total_cost int,
                             shipping_charge int,
                             handling_charge int);
```

Let's now describe these prototypes, so we are comfortable with the definitions. In these prototypes we see that some methods return an integer number, some return on values, and others return pointers to objects. In object-oriented databases, It is not uncommon to combine assignment statements with method calls. For example, the following process code will do two things, it will compute the shipping charges for the order and assign the result to a variable called my_shipping_charges:

```
my_shipping_charges =
        compute_shipping_charges(:my_order_form_OID);
```

By the same token (excuse the pun), we can also return an OID in a method call, so we can embed the OID into another object. In the following code, assume that we have defined the data type for order OID as a pointer to order. We can now do two things in a single statement. Below we are invoking the fill_order method and at the same time returning the OID of the new order object into our order_OID variable:

```
order_OID = fill_order(:cust_info);
```

What we see is that we have created a complete specification for each method, stating the name and data type of every input and output variable. Remember from Chapter 2, each of these methods will be independently tested, and the internal variable may not be known to the calling method. This is known as "information hiding," and is used when "private" variables are declared and used within the method. Remember, our goal is to make each of these methods into reusable black-boxes that can always be counted on to function properly. This is the very foundation of object method reusability.

Let us now introduce the object/relational model that we have prepared for this system. As we recall from Chapter 3, there are several components used to describe an object/relational database design. First, there is the object/relational model for the base objects (Figure 8.6). This diagram describes all of the base classes in our system, and describes the indexes, tablespaces, and the subclasses for each class definition.

Next, we take a look at the aggregate class diagram (Figure 8.7). Here we see two aggregate class definitions, their internal pointer structures and the index and tablespace information for all classes that are entirely composed of pointers to other objects.

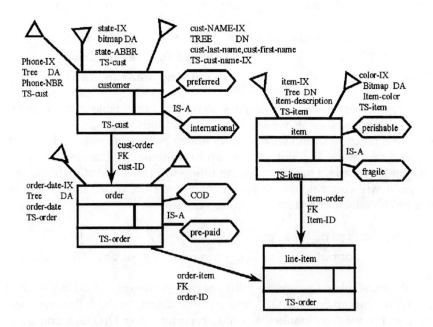

Figure 8.6 An object/relation diagram for the order processing system.

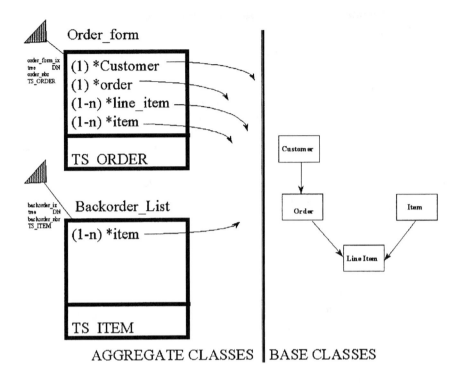

Figure 8.7 The aggregate class diagram for the order processing system.

Note that in the models we show both the base classes, as well as the aggregate classes. The question becomes, how do we map our method prototypes to these classes? Since the object–relational model represents all objects as tables, the availability of aggregate objects will now allow the coupling of aggregate methods with the "owner" table. In this fashion, an aggregate object will know how to behave based on these methods.

Automatic Method Generation

In most object-oriented and object/relational databases, the basic methods for all objects are created automatically at the time that the object class is defined. These basic methods are used when objects are created, deleted, updated and displayed, and would correspond to the INSERT, DELETE, and UPDATE SQL verbs. It is important to recognize that methods exist in several forms within the database engine:

1. Stand-alone methods (not associated with a database class)
2. Base-class methods
3. Aggregate class methods

However, more complex methods can be coupled to their target objects. For example, an order_form object might contain a method called check_payment_history which performs detailed checks into the prior payment history for the customer who is placing the order.

Now, let's take a look at our analysis of the methods that might be associated with these objects. Whenever a method of the same name appears in more than one class definition, the database will look first at the object, and traverse up the class hierarchy at runtime looking for the method.

Methods for student:

```
Display_student();
Compute_tuition();
enroll_student();
```

Methods for graduate_student;

```
assign_mentor();
computer_tuition();
update_thesis_status();
```

Methods for non_resident_students;

```
Compute_tuition();
record_transfer_statistics();
```

Methods for foreign_students;

```
compute_tuition();
```

Here we see that some methods that are unique to the subclass appear only within the subclass definition. For example, update_thesis_status would not have any meaning to an undergraduate student.

This should now provide a general method for the mapping of processes to database objects. As we have repeatedly stated, it is critical to the design of an object database that careful planning of the methods take place before the database schema is defined.

Summary

It cannot be overemphasized that it is critical to the design of a database object system that careful attention be given to the placement of methods. The concept of overloading can be very powerful, since new code can be introduced into the system with absolute certainty that no unintended side-effects will be introduced. This is because the new method will only be known to objects within that class of subclasses. Objects that belong to other class will never know that the new method exists.

Now that we understand the issues relating to the placement of methods, let's see how the object/relational model allows for the definition of aggregate objects; that is, objects that are composed of other objects.

9

SQL and Relational Databases

Dr. E. F. Codd first introduced the concept of the Structured Query Language (SQL) as part of his early work on the relational database model. Dr. Codd was famous for his creative names for his concepts and his rationale for naming SQL is no exception. For example, Codd named the process of relational database design "normalization" because President Nixon was normalizing relations with China at the time. Dr. Codd reasoned that if Nixon could normalize relations between countries then he could normalize relations between data. The naming of the relational query language as SQL is another great misnomer. One should note that SQL is not a query language. SQL performs much more than queries. It allows updates, deletes, and inserts. Also, SQL is not a language. SQL is embedded within procedural languages such as COBOL or C. Consequently, the name of Structured Query Language seemed a logical name for Dr. Codd's new tool.

Regardless of the appropriateness of the name, SQL offers three basic classes of operators, SELECT, PROJECT and JOIN. The SELECT operator serves to shrink a relational table vertically by eliminating unwanted rows. The PROJECT operator serves to shrink the table horizontally, removing unwanted columns, and the JOIN operator allowed the dynamic linking of two tables that share a common column value. Most commercial implementations of SQL do not support a PROJECT operation. In these cases, projections are achieved by specifying the columns that are desired in the output. The JOIN operation is achieved by stating the selection criteria for two tables and equating them with their common columns.

In its day, the SQL language was a revolution. It was no longer necessary to manually navigate the database one record at a time in order to resolve a database request. The new features of the SQL language included:

1. **Data Access Flexibility** — The data resides in freestanding tables, which are not hard-linked with other tables. Columns can be added to relational tables without any changes to application programs, and the addition of new data or data relationships to the data model seldom require restructuring of the tables.

2. **Declarative Data Access** — Database navigation is hidden from the programmers. When compared to a navigational language such

as CODASYL DML, which requires the programmer to know the details of the access paths, relational access is handled with an SQL optimizer. This takes care of all navigation on behalf of the user. Relational data access is a "state space" approach, whereby the user specifies the Boolean conditions for the retrieval, and the system returns the data which meets the selection criteria in the SQL statement.

3. **A Simple Conceptual Framework** — The relational database is very easy to describe, and even naive users can understand the concept of tables. Complex network diagrams, which are used to describe the structure of network and hierarchical databases, are not needed to describe a relational database.

4. **Referential Integrity (RI)** — Relational systems allow for the control of business rules with "constraints". These RI rules are used to insure that one-to-many and many-to-many relationships are enforced within the relational tables. For example, RI would ensure that a row in the CUSTOMER table could not be deleted if orders for that customer exist in the ORDER table.

One of the greatest benefits of relational databases is the concept of data independence. Because data relationships were no longer hard-linked with pointers, systems developers were able to design systems based upon business requirements with far less time being spend on physical considerations.

SQL and Objects

While these are relatively straightforward operations, they do not provide for many of the features that have become associated with the object-oriented databases, especially when dealing with abstract data types (ADT) and pointers. Many of the characteristics of SQL for relational databases are in contradiction with some of the new features of the object/relational implementations of SQL.

One of the most confounding problems in the database arena today is the reconciliation of objects with SQL. Industry experts, such as Christopher Stone, President of the Object Management Group, agree that, "So what the object database community needs...excuse me, what the object community needs...is agreement on a data model and how you pinpoint it for design, how do you build applications that are free from specific Data Manipulation Languages (DMLs). Does that mean that you extend SQL...and that's going on all over the place...to be object-oriented? Does it mean you develop an entirely new object query language? Probably not. Does it mean you just extend C++ and pray the marriage of a programming language and a database is really going to happen? I don't think that is going to happen. The writing is on the wall that it'll pretty much be an evolution of SQL. Object database technology, those extensions to SQL supporting abstract data types, and things like that will become much more prevalent over the next two to three years." For the past several years there has been a increasing effort among application developers to interface their C++ systems with relational databases.

In attempting to reconcile the object-oriented approach and relational databases, it is very important to recognize that the object-oriented approach deals with data at a much higher level than a relational database. Whereas a relational database deals with data at the level of columns and rows, an object-oriented system deals with objects, which may be any number of collections of data items. An object may be an order, an inventory list, or any real-world representation of a physical object. For example, consider an object called ORDER. ORDER is a logical object to the object-oriented system, and each ORDER will have associated data items and behaviors. Behaviors might include PLACE_ORDER, CHANGE_ORDER, and so on.

At the relational database level, an ORDER is really a consolidation of many different columns from many different tables. The customer name comes from the CUSTOMER table, order date comes from the ORDER table, quantity from the LINE_ITEM table and item description from the ITEM table. Hence, a single behavior for an object may cause changes to many tables within the relational database.

"Objects" and Relational Tables

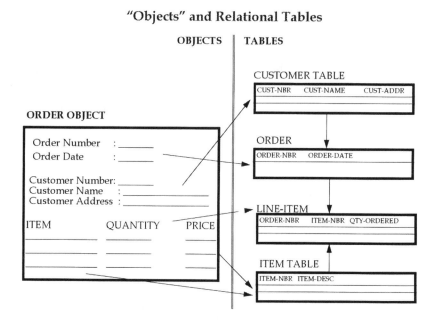

Figure 9.1 The mapping of objects to relational tables.

One of the major shortcomings of the relational database model is its inability to represent aggregate objects. All data must be decomposed into tables, and the display of an aggregate object requires a joins of the component tables at runtime. Codd suggested the use of relational "views" to represent this higher level of abstraction. For example, an SQL statement could be created an SQL view called ORDER_FORM.

```
CREATE OR REPLACE VIEW
   order_form
AS
SELECT
   customer_name,
   customer_address,
   customer_phone,
   order_nbr,
   order_date,
   item_name,
   qty_ordered
FROM
   customer,
   order,
   line_item,
   item
WHERE
   order_nbr = :hostvar;
```

The view could then be used to produce an order form in a single SQL statement without requiring the SQL syntax for joining the tables together:

```
SELECT *
FROM
   order_form
WHERE
   order_nbr = 999;
```

The relational view still misses the basic point of aggregate objects. The whole idea of data aggregation is that higher-level objects will have an independent existence instead of being rebuilt each time that the view is used. Also, relational views cannot be used for update operations. In a relational view, the row ID (RID), cannot be maintained within the subordinate tables, and consequently, UPDATE and INSERT operations are not allowed. Object behaviors such as PLACE_ORDER and CHANGE_ORDER cannot use relational views. Some researchers have suggested methods for creating "updatable" views within the relational database model, but no commercial databases have implemented support for updatable views.

SQL and the Impedance Mismatch

One of the early vendors to address this market is Persistence Software, whose object-to-relational mapping product is distinguished by its strong in-memory object caching that offsets the performance setbacks associated with translation between object and relational models (known as "impedance mismatch").

In an online object-oriented application such as a C++ program, the "impedance mismatch" between object and relational models requires encapsulated data to be mapped into a relational table for persistent storage, and then reassembled at runtime. Most implementations of this type of mapping of in-memory objects to rows in relational tables result in substantial overhead and performance degradation.

Some products alleviate this problem with their large object caches, which retain highly used business objects, along with their encapsulated data, in memory. This avoids the overhead associated with reassembly of objects from the underlying relational tables, as well as the delays associated with repeatedly reading from disk.

SQL and Encapsulation Violation

Encapsulation is used in non-database object-oriented applications to ensure that all operations are performed through the programmer-defined interface, and that the data will never be modified outside of the application shell. But what about ad-hoc query and update? It appears that any declarative database language such as SQL, which allows "external" retrieval and update, does not follow the dictates of encapsulation, and is therefore inconsistent with object-oriented database management.

For example, a relational database could be defined to have a behavior called ADD_LINE_ITEM, which checks inventory levels for an item and adds an item to an order only if sufficient stock is available. This behavior insures that orders are not entered for out-of-stock items. With a language such as

SQL, the object-oriented behavior could be bypassed, and LINE_ITEM records could be added without any regard for inventory levels.

Because encapsulation and SQL are incompatible, the only conclusion one reach is that encapsulation does not apply to object-oriented databases because declarative languages violate the principle. In addition, we might also conclude that declarative languages cannot be used within a true object-oriented database because all objects must be their methods to gain access.

The most important feature of the relational database is the ability to isolate the data from the data relationships, and to eliminate the "pointers" that were used by hierarchical and network databases to establish relationships. In a relational database, two tables that have a relationship are defined with a primary key and a foreign key. These keys can be used at runtime to dynamically join the tables.

SQL was a tremendous benefit to programmers because it removed the requirements of the database that the use of the system "navigate" the data structures. As we know, SQL is called "declarative" in the sense that the user needs only specify the desired data, and the database engine will take care of the navigation. Hierarchical, network, and object-oriented databases require the programmer to navigate the data structures to get his selected data. With SQL the age of end-user access became a reality. Users began to use SQL to access their information without programmer intervention. The term "declarative," in this context, means that the actual navigation path to the data is hidden from the user, and the user "declares" a solution set that meets her selection criteria. The SQL optimizer would determine the proper access for the data and handle all of the database navigation.

Problems with SQL and Objects

There are several constructs within the SQL language that conflict with object-oriented databases. The most obvious is the requirement that SQL serves as an ad-hoc query facility.

These problems fit into the categories of abstract data typing, encapsulation and methods, and the realm of pointers. All of these constructs are very foreign to SQL and special extensions have been created to allow for the implementation of these constructs.

SQL and Abstract Data Types

Another problem relates to the SQL CREATE TABLE statement. Object-oriented systems allow the concept of abstract data typing. Programmers may create their own data types, which become indistinguishable from the system-defined data types. For example, an object-oriented programmer could define a data type of BOOLEAN, which would be treated by the system just a CHAR or INTEGER data type. Relational technology does not have a facility for self-defining new data types. The new object/relational databases, however, do allow for data items to be created and used with the CREATE TYPE constructs which were discussed in earlier chapters.

Of course, there are also SQL extensions to allow for the creation and implementation of these abstract data types. The following SQL is used to create a customer table. Note that two of the components—full_name and full_address—are abstract data types, and the entire customer table has been encapsulated into an ADT called customer_stuff;

```
CREATE TYPE
    full_address (
        street_address      varchar(20),
        city_name           varchar(20),
        state_name          char(2),
        zip_code            number(9));


CREATE TYPE
    full_name (
        first_name          varchar(20),
        MI                  char(1),
        last_name           varchar(30));


CREATE TYPE
    customer_stuff (
        customer_ID         number(6),
        cust_full_name      full_name,
        cust_full_address   full_address));


CREATE TABLE CUSTOMER of customer_stuff;
```

Once the ADTs have been defined, SQL has been extended to allow for the use of sub-typing to address those data components that are nested within larger data types. For example, we could use the following SQL to select the zip code for a particular customer:

```
SELECT
  customer_stuff.full_address.zip_code
FROM
  CUSTOMER
WHERE
  customer_ID = 764645;
```

While dealing with ADTs is a relatively trivial extension to SQL there are many other new constructs that need to be addressed.

Object SQL and Encapsulation

One of the basic constructs of object-oriented programming is encapsulation. Encapsulation is defined as the ability to access objects only via their behaviors. This is contradictory to a basic principle of the relational database model—data independence—which says that any data may be accessed in an ad hoc, independent fashion.

At first glance, it seems that these two concepts cannot be reconciled because it would be impossible to have data tables which are independent of the application, while at the same time supporting encapsulation, which tightly-couples the objects and their behaviors. However, these concepts are not contradictory. Because the behaviors are stored in the database, they are not external, and will not jeopardize the independence of applications from data.

For example, one could only access the CREDIT_RATING field in the CUSTOMER table by invoking the PLACE_ORDER behavior. The SQL language, of course, would allow access and update to any data items that are allowed within the system security tables. Any authorized user could view the credit rating of a customer without ever invoking an object-oriented method.

Another conceptual limitation of SQL, which has legitimate ramifications for object-oriented databases, is the inability of SQL to associate a behavior with a data item. SQL requires that the properties of an object and its operational semantics be coded within an external entity—the application program. Also, SQL has no built-in method for incorporating behaviors into tables. However, there is a solution to this problem. Many of the object/relational database vendors have created "methods" for database objects that have a one-for-one correspondence with the SQL operators. For example, a database might automatically create a method called insert_customer, which would invoke the appropriate SQL statement to insert a row into a customer table. A database might automatically create methods to insert, update and delete rows from the target table, much as C++ allows for constructors and destructors for objects. While this works fine for a simple operation, there is still a problem for more sophisticated methods that access and alter more than one data column.

Many of the built-in functions of SQL also violate the encapsulation rule. For example, instead of writing a method to compute the gross pay for an employee, we could directly use SQL to perform this operation, thereby bypassing the method:

```
SELECT
  hours_worked*payrate
FROM
  timesheet, payrates
WHERE
  emp_id = 123
AND
  week = '03/98';
```

The same is true when using the SUM, AVG and any one of the dozens of other SQL functions that are offered by the major relational database vendors.

SQL and Pointers

One of the greatest mismatches with SQL and objects lies in the arena of pointers. The introduction of pointers into the relational model has led to a situation where the declarative nature of SQL is being radically changed.

For example, the use of the DEREF operator in the new object/relational SQL allows a SQL statement to dereference a row pointer, essentially navigating from one table to the next table. Rather than relying on the SQL optimizer to take care of the database access, the developers now have the option of embedding SQL statements into their programs that will allow them to navigate through the database, visiting tables that have been linked together with pointers. This is a very foreign idea for most SQL developers but it is now a reality.

For example, the following SQL could be used to navigate from a customer to the order rows for the customer:

```
SELECT
  DEREF(order_list)
FROM
  CUSTOMER
WHERE
  customer_id = "JONES";
```

This would be the equivalent to the traditional SQL:

```
SELECT
  order_stuff
FROM
  CUSTOMER, ORDER
WHERE
  customer_id = "JONES"
AND
  customer_ID = order_ID;
```

The SQL becomes even more confounding when we start dealing with the more abstract uses of pointers in a relational/object model. As we recall from earlier chapters, these pointer constructs use object-IDs (OID) and include some very abstract data structures:

- Pointers to individual rows in other tables.
- Repeating groups of pointers to rows.
- Pointers to arrays of pointers to rows.
- Pointers to whole tables.
- Multidimensional arrays of pointers.

Many of the relational vendors have extended their SQL syntax to provide the following constructs to deal with pointers:

DEREF — This SQL operator accepts an OID and returns the contents of the row that the OID points to:

```
SELECT
  DEREF(order_oid)
FROM
  CUSTOMER;
```

CAST and MULTISET — These SQL operators castsa multiple input data stream into the appropriate data types for the SQL operation:

```
INSERT INTO
    COURSE (STUDENT_LIST)
    (CAST
        (MULTISET
            (SELECT
                student_name,
                student_address,
                grade
            FROM
                GRADE, STUDENT
            WHERE
                GRADE.course_name = 'CS101'
                AND
                GRADE.student_name =
                        STUDENT.student_name
            )
        )
    );
```

With all of these new pointer constructs and extensions to SQL, it will be several years before the mainstream programming community arrives at a general agreement about the use of pointer-based navigation within SQL programming.

SQL and Inheritance

As we recall from Chapter 7, the object/relational database allows the developer to create a class hierarchy of related data items, where each item in the class hierarchy is a subtype of another data type. These types of IS-A relationships, while valid from a data modeling viewpoint, do not have a simple implementation in object/relational databases. Since most object/relational databases do not support hierarchical relationships, it is impossible to directly represent the fact that a database entity has subentities.

Once an object has been instantiated, the data items within the object have been defined and the object may be used within SQL to retrieve the data items. The problem is that a separate table must exist for all subclasses within the class hierarchy, since each my have separate data items. Therefore, if we have a class hierarchy with ten separate classes, there we may have ten separate tables to hold the instantiated objects. This can make the SQL more complicated, especially since we must know the type of the object when we make the query. In the following example, we are querying the data items from a luxury_sedan vehicle, and we must know that it is of the type "luxury_sedan" in order to formulate the query:

```
SELECT
    vehicle_number,
    registration_number,
    number_of_doors,
    type_of_leather_upholstery
FROM
    LUXURY_SEDAN
WHERE
    sedan.key = 8383635;
```

Perhaps future implementations of object/relational databases may remove the SQL restriction of having to explicitly specify the target table by name, but today there is no way that any SQL optimizer will be able to tell the sub-type of the target object without some kind of a hint.

Summary

Now that we have addressed the basic issues relating to SQL and objects, let's take a look at how many of the database developers are interfacing objects with SQL by developing object-oriented applications that use relational database to store their object information.

10

Interfacing C++ with Relational Databases

With the increasing popularity of object-oriented technology, many relational database shops want the ability to take advantage of C++ applications while continuing to use their relational databases. The widespread acceptance of object technology has lead many companies to the conclusion that they must embrace object orientation, but they remain skeptical about the maturity of the object-oriented database (OODB) technology. Many companies are averse to risk and do not want to embrace one of the nascent OODB offerings, and they cannot wait for the object/relational databases. Other companies who have invested millions of dollars in relational database systems want to continue with a relational architecture without missing out on the benefits of object technology.

When interfacing object-oriented languages with relational databases there is a problem encountered when using SQL with a general-purpose object-oriented programming language, which causes an impedance mismatch.

There are two aspects to this impedance mismatch between SQL and objects:

1. A difference in programming paradigms, i.e., between a declarative language such as SQL and an imperative language such as C++.

2. A mismatch in the type systems, causing a loss of information to occur at the interface. The DML in most relational database systems does not support the computational completeness needed to express complex mathematical manipulations of data common to engineering design. OODBMS, however, provide database extensions to computationally complete programming languages, like C++ and SmallTalk, that are capable of handling complex mathematcal manipulations typical of large-scale programs that are common to engineering design.

Regardless of the promises of the relational database vendors, there are those who wish to enjoy the benefits of a robust and mature database while continuing to pursue object technology. However, there are drastic differences between object technology and relational databases. In a true OODB, object persistence—storing the object—is achieved by calling a method for the object that makes the object reside in permanent disk storage. In other words, persistence is just another method that is associated with the object. This is very different from a relational database where a row can be inserted from any program at any time.

Unlike relational databases, the OODBMS offerings also have a very tight coupling of the database with the host programming language. Consequently, OODBMS generally are designed with a specific language in mind, such as C++ or SmallTalk. Relational databases such as Oracle are language independent, and many Oracle shops are having success writing C++ applications and running them through the Pro*C precompiler.

The Method

There are many different approaches to using a relational database with an object-oriented application, and this text offers only one of many different approaches. However, all of the approaches involve some common factors and procedures. The goal of "stuffing" an object into a relational table generally involves the following steps:

1. Document the object structure for the application using Booch diagrams, Rumbaugh diagrams, etc.
2. Review all methods with the C++ application.
3. Review the object navigation and create logical pointers.
4. Add object extensions to manage internal pointers.
5. For each class, map the data items and pointers to a relational table.
6. Write C/SQL snippets to move the object data and pointers into the table row.
7. Rewrite the I/O to utilize the logical pointers.

While these steps are not exhaustive, they describe the major steps in converting a C++ application to function with a relational database. While these are the steps, it must be stressed that every application is different. A C++ application that uses logical pointers, avoids "arrays of pointers" and isolates object I/O is very easy to back-end into a relational database. On the other hand, a C++ application that uses physical object addresses as pointers; i.e., capturing the address of an object and embedding it in another object to establish a relationship, utilizes arrays of pointers, and has separate I/O statements within each method can be very difficult to back-end to a relational database.

This chapter illustrates some of these issues and provide examples on how to write C++ code that can utilize relational engines for persistent object storage.

The Problem of Pointers: Logical vs. Physical

The usage of pointers to navigate object relationships within a traditional object-oriented application may also have to be reworked if one plans to use a relational database. In a non-persistent C++ applications, an object is created with the NEW operator, memory is allocated and the address of that object is captured. Of course, this address is not permanent, and a subsequent run of the application may find the same object in another memory address. For this reason, a method must be determined to replace the "physical" memory address pointers with "logical" pointers to the object (Figure 10.1).

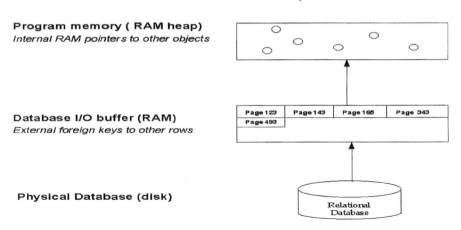

C++/RDBMS has two sets of pointers

Program memory (RAM heap)
Internal RAM pointers to other objects

Database I/O buffer (RAM)
External foreign keys to other rows

| Page 123 | Page 143 | Page 165 | Page 343 |
| Page 493 | | | |

Physical Database (disk)

Relational Database

Figure 10.1   The duality of pointers.

Logical pointers generally assign an object-ID, which is called an "OID" (rhymes with "annoyed"). The OID is associated to an object when it is instantiated, the OO term for object creation, and will use this OID as a logical pointer when navigating data relationships. There are many ways to create logical OIDs. Some OODBMS make their OIDs by relating to the logical container, similar to a database "page", in which the object resides, including a byte offset into the container. For example, if a CUSTOMER object hashes to container number 123 and is assigned space number 4 within that container, then the OID would have a value of 123-4.

The question of access to relational data is simplified if we mark a data item as being the primary key for the object. In this fashion, we can always retrieve the object from disk using SQL, and then reestablish the OID after we have reinstantiated the object.

The main goal of this technique is to take an object and stuff its data and pointers into a row of a relational table. Of course, the relational table will not be able to make any sense of these pointers, and the relational table structure would not contain any of the "foreign keys" that we are accustomed to using for relational navigation. SQL joins cannot be used against these tables, but queries against individual tables can still be performed.

In other words, an object uses internal navigation through its pointers to other objects, while the relational database must join primary keys with foreign keys to establish a relationship. Compare the following navigation between C++ objects and the relational equivalent.

C++

```
ordersForCustomer() { // list all orders for a
    customer

cout << "\n\nOrder summary for customer "
    <<custName<< " \n";
int i;
for(i=0;i<orderCount;i++) {
    cout << "\n Order = " << orderList[i]
        ->orderNum;
};
```

SQL

```
Select order_number from customer, order
where customer_num = :custno and
customer.customer_num = order.customer_num
```

Here we see that the navigation between objects is quite different from the navigation between rows in a relational database. We must keep in mind that associations between objects are pointers to addresses in the memory of the C++ program. Since each object pointer refers to the RAM memory location of an associated object, we must address the question about how to create "parallel universes" of associations, one for the relational database and another for the in-memory objects.

At first glance it may be tempting to simply store the in-memory pointers for the objects into rows of a relational table. These in-memory addresses are established by C++ in the object constructor, and the actual memory address is dependent upon the prior objects that the program has constructed. However, since the base register for the C++ program will be different for each execution of the program, we can never count on these in-memory addresses to be the same between executions of the program. In other words, the in-memory address for the customer ABC object will always be different, each time the constructor is invoked.

When customer ABC is constructed for the first time, we must store the object in our relational database, independent of any internal C++ pointers. When the object is retrieved by a later execution of the C++ program, the row is called from disk into the database buffer, and then transferred into C++ memory with a memory allocation, using the C++ malloc or new operators. It is safe to assume that each time an object is retrieved from disk and allocated to the C++ program, it will have a new memory address. So then, how can we manage internal associations between objects?

Consider the following example. Here we have one customer, ABC, who has two orders, order 123 and order 456. The customer object will have an internal array of pointers to orders, and will store the in-memory pointers for order 123 and order 456. Each order, in turn, will store an up-level object pointer to point to customer ABC as shown in Figure 10.2.

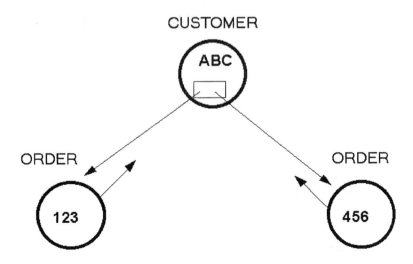

Figure 10.2 Pointer structures between objects

Next, we will want to make these objects persistent, and store them as rows in our relational database. We will want to store customer ABC as a row in the customer table, and orders 123 and 456 will each store as rows in the order table. Since we will store "ABC" as the primary key for the customer and as a foreign key for each order, we can be assured that the logical relationship between these relational rows will be maintained. It would be senseless to try to store the array of order pointers, since their values would be meaningless to a subsequent run, but we could store information that there are exactly two orders for this customer.

But what happens when customer ABC is retrieved by a subsequent run of our C++ program? We can easily use SQL to retrieve the customer row from the table and malloc space in the programs memory for customer ABC, but how can we establish the pointers to orders 123 and 456? They have not yet been retrieved, and will not have addresses until we manually call them in from the database and reinstantiate them. At this point, customer ABC's array of pointers to orders contains nothing but NULL pointers, since the orders have not been retrieved from memory. However, we could write a routine that would check to see if the pointer is NULL, and then go to the database and retrieve all orders for the customer with an SQL statement. In this case we know that each order is identified by a unique order number, but it may not always be so easy to find a key for the subobjects. In either case, we must somehow keep the relational keys for each order that has been placed by the customer. There are two approaches to this:

1. Create a second array in each customer object to hold the relational keys for each order. This array would parallel the array of pointers to orders in the customer object.
2. Create a global table of array references with the following fields:

OWNER_TABLE	OWNER_KEY	MEMBER_TABLE	MEMBER_KEY
customer	ABC	order	123
customer	ABC	order	456

3. Remove all arrays of pointer, and use linked-list structures.

Using method 1 or 2, orders 123 and 456 can now be brought into the memory of the C++ program by calling the appropriate SQL. After the SQL has returned the rows, the objects are reinstantiated and the pointers reassigned to the customer and order objects.

Identifying Objects

This method is fine for establishing relationships between objects, but how do we uniquely identify customer ABC? Just as the object database required an object-ID for each object, we must create a unique ID for each row in the database.

Some OODBMS systems assign arbitrary unique numbers to identify an object of each class, and still others use a hashing algorithm to determine a logical key. Another method of OID creation is to maintain your own OIDs. Some programmers create a data integer in the object called objectNameKey, and increment this key each time that an object is instantiated. This key can be stored in a relational database as the primary key and is also used as a pseudo-pointer for any objects that have relationships with the target object.

Another method is popular with users who have Oracle relational databases that allow selection of the row-ID (called the "rid"). They insert a row and then re-select the row obtaining the rid into the C++ application. For example, the SQL to store customer ABC would read:

```
INSERT INTO CUSTOMER VALUES ("ABC", "123 First St.",
    "Anywhere, NJ");

SELECT RID INTO :HOLD_RID FROM CUSTOMER WHERE
    CUST_ID = 'ABC'.

UPDATE CUSTOMER
SET RID_KEY = :HOLD_RID
WHERE CUST_ID = 'ABC';
```

Pointer Architectures

There is another problem relating to the pointer architectures of C++ applications. Unlike databases that conform to standard pointer architectures, such as the CODASYL DBTG model, object-oriented applications are unconstrained by any "conventions" or rules, about a uniform method for establishing pointer relationships.

The Committee on Development of Applied Symbolic Languages (CODASYL) formed a database task group (the DBTG) in the 1970s to address the problem of diverse database standards. The CODASYL DBTG was commissioned to develop a set of rules, or a model for database management systems, just as the ODMG group is doing with object-oriented databases. The CODASYL DBTG developed what is called the "network model" for databases. The CODASYL model became the framework for a new generation of commercial database systems such as the IDMS database from Cullinane Corporation and the MDBS2 database.

Regardless of conventions, there are two pointer methods that are predominant in commercial systems and a discussion of the merits of each method will clarify the issues.

The first pointer method closely follows the CODASYL DBTG model in which each relationship, sometimes called a "set," contains circular two-way linked list pointers representing NEXT, PRIOR, and OWNER. For a many-to-many relationship such as ORDER and ITEM we see linkages to a junction object. This is shown in Figure 10.3.

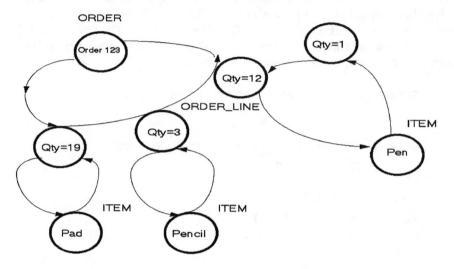

Figure 10.3   A set occurrence diagram.

In this diagram, we can follow the NEXT pointer and see that order 123 contains 19 items and then follow the owner pointer to see that these items are Pads. We can then continue along the NEXT chain to an object with a quantity of "3", and follow the owner pointer in the other set to see that these items are pencils. Continuing along the original NEXT chain we hit 12 items, and following the owner pointer, we see that they are 12 pens. Conversely, we could navigate from the pen object to see all orders that contain pens. Following the pens NEXT pointer, we see a quantity of 1 and we could follow the owner pointer of this object to get order 456 (not shown). Continuing along the pen's NEXT chain we encounter 12 pens, and following the owner pointer we see that it is in order 123.

With this two-way linked list approach, very long relationships can be represented without the overhead of having a very long array of pointers in the owner object. For example, if a customer places an average of 5000 orders, the resulting array in the owner record would be extremely large (> 2000 bytes). We also have some control over what the relational database folks call referential integrity (RI). By using RI we can enforce business rules, for example, no orders may be placed unless they are from a valid customer, or no customer may be deleted if they have outstanding orders. The two-way linked list approach helps us to enforce these business rules. In the first example, an ORDER object cannot be inserted unless "currency" has been established with a CUSTOMER because the linked-list algorithm requires the establishment of NEXT and PRIOR pointer in adjacent objects. In the delete example, a CUSTOMER destructor may not be called if the NEXT pointer points to a valid ORDER object.

Another popular method for representing relationships is to create an array of pointers in the owner object. This array contains one bucket for each member object in the relationship. Each member object in turn contains a pointer back to the owner object. Figure 10.4 illustrates this type of pointer architecture.

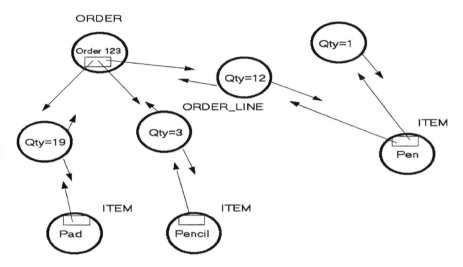

Figure 10.4   Using arrays of pointers.

The method of using arrays of pointers has some benefits over two-way linked lists. If the sets are small, say less than 100 members for each owner, sorting of members can be achieved without re-linking all of the members. For example, if we have 100 orders for a customer and we wish to sort the array of pointers such that the orders are retrieved in ORDER_DATE sequence, we can easily sweep the orders and internally sort the array into the desired order, all without altering any of the ORDER objects. This type of pointer twizzling can be very useful over the traditional linked-list method in which the pointers within each object would need to be readjusted.

Unfortunately, the concept of "arrays of pointers" is very difficult to map into a relational table. Most relational databases do not support repeating groups within tables and there is no direct way to represent an array within a relational table.

When this pointer architecture is encountered there are two alternatives: the application can be rewritten to employ linked-lists or another relational table can be created to hold the array of pointers. Neither solution is ideal, and it is often easier to rewrite the application with linked-list pointer structures.

Remember, the idea is to create a parallel set of logical pointers to be used by the relational tables, but we will not need to alter any of the existing pointer structures in the C++ application. However, it can be very confusing when the in-memory object navigation is performed with arrays of pointers while the access to persistent object is done with linked-list pointers.

The most elegant solution is to have the C++ application and the relational database using a similar pointer architecture. This way, when an object is requested (if it is not already in memory), a common "call" can be made to the relational database to fetch the object.

Aggregate Objects

Another feature of the object model is the concept of aggregation. Because object technology systems use embedded pointers to establish their data relationships and because they pre-assemble aggregate objects, they will almost always out-perform a relational database, but they attain this speed by sacrificing the ability to dynamically establish new relationships between existing database records. In other words, object-oriented databases achieve their speed at the expense of data independence. In a relational database, information is "assembled" from independent tables at the time of the query. Object-oriented advocates state that this approach is analogous to assembling your automobile when you want to travel, and then disassembling the car after you have completed your trip. An object technology system pre-establishes each of the data relationship with embedded pointers.

When using C++ with a relational database, the question of aggregate objects must be addressed. In general, an aggregate object will consist of data items and pointers to the sub-objects that comprise the aggregate. Consider the following order form:

> Order Form:
> ABC Computer Supplies
> Order Number: 123
> Date: 3/1/97

> Customer:
> ISS Chemicals
> 124 First Ave.
> Anywhere, NY, 11253

ITEM	Description	QTY	Unit price	Total price
z242	Pen	10	1.49	14.99
h484	Pencils	50	2.00	10.00
u883	Pads	10	3.49	34.90

Total Price	$ 59.89
Sales Tax	$ 5.98
Discount	$ 11.96
Amount Due	$ 65.87

While this object has subcomponents, the discount may be time-dependent and is unique to this aggregate. Therefore we would need to be stored in the object database. It is a good idea to create an item-map that shows each of the sub-assemblies, and identifies their unique keys. If we were using a global table to store this information, the rows would look like this:

OWNER_TABLE	OWNER_KEY	MEMBER_TABLE	MEMBER_KEY
order-form	123‖3/1/97	order	123
order-form	123‖3/1/97	line-item	123‖h484
order-form	123‖3/1/97	line-item	123‖u883

Designing the Overall Object Architecture

Some designers of C++ applications create a class called "persistent" and have all classes that will be stored in the relational database inherit from this class. There are two advantages to this approach. The primary advantage to this approach is that the designer can encapsulate the code that is used to make an object persistent. Also, there will be times when the C++ application must make an object persistent in the relational database and other times when the object may not need to be persistent. An example would be runtime objects that are used to drive the processes, but are never stored.

Conversion to Relational Databases

To illustrate the steps in conversion to relational databases, consider the following sample C++ application that manages customers, orders, and items.

STEP 1:   Review the object structure of the application.

This first step is to diagram the objects and indicate all relationships between the objects. The relationships may be one-to-many (1:M) as in the case between CUSTOMER and ORDER, many-to-many (M:N) as in the case between ORDER and ITEM, or a recursive many-to-many as in the case between ITEM and COMPONENT (Figure 10.5).

E/R Model: Guttbaum's Hamburgers

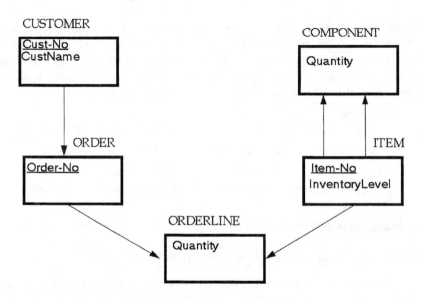

Figure 10.5   An entity/relation model.

In this diagram we see the following data relationships between the objects:

> Each customer may place many orders; an order belongs to only one customer.
>
> Each order may contain many items; an item may participate in many orders.
>
> An item may consist of many items; an item may be a part of many items.

We see that CUSTOMER-ORDER is a one-to-many relationship because a CUSTOMER object may have many orders, but each ORDER object belongs to a single CUSTOMER object.

Also note that each ORDER object has a many-to-many relationship to ITEM objects via the junction object ORDERLINE. Each ORDER object has many items, and each ITEM object participates on many orders. We see that the ORDERLINE object contains a data item, QUANTITY that applies only to this joining between orders and items. To illustrate, the data item "Quantity" makes no sense when applied to a single item (i.e., what is the quantity for pens?), and it makes no sense when applied only to a single order (i.e. what is the quantity in order #123?), but it makes sense when applied to both objects (i.e. what is the quantity of pens in order #123?). Consequently, a junction object has been established that contains pointers to the owner ITEM object and the ORDER object. Since the primary reason for the existence of the ORDERLINE object is to establish this many-to-many relationship, the only data item in the ORDERLINE object is QUANTITY.

The recursive many-to-many relationship is seen between the ITEM object and the component object. Essentially an ITEM object many be composed of many other ITEM objects, while the same ITEM object may exist as a sub-component in a still larger ITEM. For example, a carburetor may have components (that are also items) such as VALVES and GASKETS, while the carburetor may be a subitem in a larger assembly such as the ENGINE object. This type of relationship is established with two arrays of pointers in each ITEM object, one for the HAS-PARTS relationship and another for the IS-A-PART relationship. The COMPONENT object has two sets of owner pointers, one for the HAS-PART owner and another for the IS-A-PART owner. COMPONENT may be created as a separate class or eliminated by using arrays of pointers in the ITEM object. To conform to the relational model COMPONENT has been added as a junction object.

STEP 2:   Review the methods associated with each object.

Let's also assume that the following methods are attached to the entities (objects). For simplicity, only some basic methods have been shown. A real application will have many additional methods.

MESSAGE	FROM	TO
placeOrder()	customer	order
computeDiscount()	order	customer
checkInventory()	orderLine	item
ordersForCustomer()	USER	customer
ItemsInOrder()	order	orderLine
checkCredit()	USER	customer

Once the message hierarchy has been determined, you can extend the descriptions to include the activities for each method:

CUSTOMER METHODS:

    customer (constructor method)

        adds custName to customer object.

    ordersForCustomer()

        lists the orderNum for all orders associated with this
            customer

ORDER METHODS:

    order (constructor method)

        add orderNum to order object.

        establishes pointer to customer placing order.

        establishes pointer in customer object to point to this
            order.

    itemsInOrder()

    Lists all item names, prices, quantities and total cost for all
        items in an order.

ITEM METHODS:

    item(constructor)

        adds itemName field to item object

ORDERLINE METHOD:

    orderline(constructor)

        adds quantity data to orderline object.

        establishes pointer to item object.

        establishes pointer to order object.

        establishes pointer in item to point to orderline object.

        establishes pointer in order object to point to orderline.

In the real world, some methods may be nested within other methods. For example, a PlaceOrder method has CheckInventory, addItems, and ComputeOrderTotal as submethods. For example:

    order (constructor method)

        CheckInventory

            PlaceBackOrder

        AddItems

        ComputeOrderTotal

            ComputeDiscount

When reviewing the methods, special attention needs to be paid to the constructors for each class because this will be where the SQL will be placed to insert the object as a row in a relational table. We also need to review all methods that navigate between objects because these will need to be changed to include SQL SELECT statements (if the object is not already in memory).

STEP 3: Review object navigation and add relational keys.

It is far easier to incorporate a relational database if the application has all of its I/O modules isolated. A poorly written C++ application is very cumbersome, if not impossible to back-end into a relational database. The basic object constructors and destructors are easy to alter, but the difficulty occurs when the objects are navigated because there will be many places that need to be changed.

If the C++ application is being written from scratch, it is nice to have only two I/O modules, a getOwner(class * objectname) for traversing from member to owner and a getMember(class * objectname) for traversing from owner to member. This type of access accepts the object name as a parameter and insures that all object navigation in the entire application is performed through a global method. Consequently, the global method is all that must change when migrating to a relational database.

A review of our example C++ application (see appendix) reveals several problems:

1. Arrays of pointers are used to establish all relationships between objects.
2. Pointer navigation is done within several methods.

If we are going to alter this C++ program to store objects into a relational table then we must create some "logical" pointers to replace the physical pointers for object navigation. These logical pointers will also serve as a primary key for the rows in the relational table. The use of pointers to establish object relationships will also need to be changed to utilize a "logical" pointer rather than a physical memory address. With parallel pointers, a second set of logical pointers can refer to the rows in the relational tables, and the rows can be retrieved with the logical pointer serving as the primary key for the table.

For example, the following ORDER constructor set two pointers, one to establish a pointer from CUSTOMER to ORDER and another to establish a pointer from the order to the CUSTOMER:

```
order(customer &cust,int ordnum) {      // order
          constructor
  cout << "\nCreating order " << ordnum << "\n";
  itemCount = 0;
  orderNum = ordnum;                     // set the order
          number
  cust.orderList[cust.orderCount++] =
     this;                               // set cust ->
          order
  custOwner = &cust;                     // set order ->
          cust
pointer
  };
```

This code could be rewritten to embed an SQL call that stores the order information in a table, but what shall we use as a primary key? The answer is to create a global variable to track and assign primary keys to each object.

For example, the C++ application may have:

```
     int nextCustKey = 0;
     int nextOrderKey = 0;
```

These global variables will keep track of the last primary key for each class and the last key that has been assigned to a row of a table. As new objects are instantiated (created), the next key is used as the OID for the object.

For example, to add a new customer object to a customer table, we can add the following code to the customer constructor:

```
     // access global variable and increment
     int custKey = nextCustKey++;

     // convert the pointer to char to a character
     char namefield[81];
     strcpy(namefield,custName);

     EXEC SQL;
        INSERT INTO CUSTOMER VALUES ( custKey,
           namefield)
        COMMIT
     END-EXEC;
```

Now, whenever a new customer object is stored, a corresponding row is stored into the relational table named CUSTOMER. Of course, we have not yet addressed the issue of pointers, but they will be handled in the following text.

STEP 4:   Replace all arrays of in-memory pointers with persistent linked-lists.

When using a relational database with C++ objects, referential integrity will not be an issue. In other words, there is no need to define any relationships between the relational tables; the relationships will be maintained by pointers that are stuffed into fields of the relational tables, and the C++ runtime application will de-reference the pointers and fetch to desired rows. Consequently, SQL JOIN statements are useless with this type of approach and all object navigation will be performed within the methods that are associated with the C++ class.

Since there will be no joining of tables there is no need to create any fields in the relational tables for foreign keys. We will, of course, need to create a primary key for each table.

Remember that the C++ pointers (i.e., objectname *) are pointers to transient memory. Consequently, we will need to create mirrored (parallel) pointer structures that contain logical (not physical) pointers and then use these pointers for the relational database.

If the class structures in the C++ application contain an array of pointers (please review sample application in appendix) we have a problem (Figure 10.6). Most relational databases do not allow for repeating groups (arrays) within a table. Our other choices are to create numbered atomic fields (i.e., key1, key2, key3), or to create another table solely for the purpose of holding this array of pointers. It seems unnecessarily complex to create another table just to track the array of pointers to the member records, but it can be done if the subordinate table carries the owner table name as a foreign key. This subordinate table must also contain the sequence within the array so that the objects can be retrieved in their original order.

Another method that is more straightforward is to create a BLOB (binary large object) within the relational table, and string the array of logical pointers into this BLOB. Many databases define a BLOB as a LONG VARCHAR or a LONG RAW datatype. LONG VARCHAR is generally used for text data and computes the length of the string for you when it is stored into the table. But beware if you are using numeric integers as logical keys. Some relational databases interrogate numeric data and treat the first null byte as the end of the string. If you use LONG RAW you can get around this limitation, but you must manually compute the length of the numeric array when storing it into the table.

Because of these kinds of problems it is usually easier to rewrite the persistent object navigation with linked-lists. This is what has been done in the

Relational representation of an array of pointers.

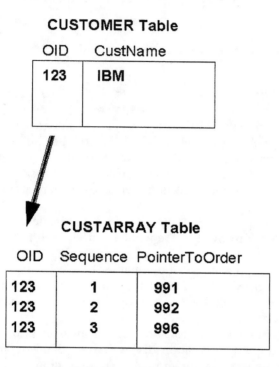

CUSTOMER Table

OID	CustName
123	IBM

CUSTARRAY Table

OID	Sequence	PointerToOrder
123	1	991
123	2	992
123	3	996

Figure 10.6   Representing relationships with arrays of pointers

following example, and the arrays of pointers have been replaced with a single pointer to the first member object and we will need to rewrite the navigation methods for the persistent objects.

In the example below, we have rewritten the class descriptions for CUSTOMER and ORDER to use one-way linked lists. The application will still function, and the pointer information will be much easier to write in parallel for the relational database access.

```
BEFORE classes (using array of pointers):

class customer {

  public:
    char * custName;
    order ** orderList;          // pointers to
          orders for this customer
    int orderCount;
```

```
   customer(char * p) {            // constructor for
        customer
     cout << "creating customer " << p << "\n";
     int l;
     l = strlen(p);                // get length of
        string

     custName = new char[l+1];  // get space for
        customer name
     if (!custName) { cout << "allocation error!\n";
        exit(1);}
     strcpy(custName,p);           // copy in the
        customer name
     orderCount = 0;
   };
};

class order {

  public:
  customer * custOwner;          // pointer to
        customer placing order
  orderline ** itemList;         // pointers to line
        items in the order
  int orderNum, itemCount;

  order(customer &cust, int ordnum) {
                                 // order
        constructor
     cout << "\nCreating order " << ordnum << "\n";
     itemCount = 0;
     orderNum = ordnum;          // set the order
        number
     cust.orderList[cust.orderCount++] = this;
                                 // set cust ->
        order
     custOwner = &cust;          // set order->
        customer pointer
  };
```

After modification to use one-way linked lists:

```
class customer {
public:
  char * custName;
  order * orderPtr;              // pointer to
        first order for customer
  int orderCount;
  customer(char * p){            // constructor
        for customer
    cout << "creating customer " << p << "\n";
    int l;
    l = strlen(p);               // get length of
        string

    custName = new char[l+1];    // get space for
        customer name
    if (!custName) { cout << "allocation error!\n";
        exit(1);}

    strcpy(custName,p);          // copy in the
        customer name
    orderCount = 0;
    orderPtr = NULL;             // set pointer to
        null
  };
    customer::ordersForCustomer();// list all
        orders for a customer
};

class order {

  public:
  customer * custOwner;          // pointer to
        customer placing order
  Orderline * itemPtr;           // pointer to
        next line item in the order
```

```
order * nextOrder;              // pointer to
        next prder in list
int orderNum, itemCount;

order(customer &cust, int ordnum) {// order
        constructor
  cout << "\nCreating order " << ordnum << "\n";
  itemCount = 0;
  orderNum = ordnum;            // set the order
        number
  nextOrder = cust.orderPtr;
    cust.orderPtr = this;       // set cust ->
        order
  custOwner = &cust;            // set order->
        customer pointer
  cust.orderCount++;
};
// Note that the end of the list of orders is
        marked by a NULL pointer.
```

Now that we have changed the pointer architecture, we can begin to change the retrieval methods. For example, look at the ordersForCustomer method before the pointer change and after the insertion of one-way linked lists.

Before: (with array of pointers in CUSTOMER)

```
ordersForCustomer() {           // list all
        orders for a customer

  cout << "\n\nOrder summary for customer " <<
        custName << " \n";
  int i;
  for(i=0;i<orderCount;i++) {
    cout << "\n Order = " << orderList[i]->order-
Num;
  };
  return 0;
};
```

After: (Modification to use one-way linked lists)

```
customer::ordersForCustomer() { // list all
orders for a customer

    cout << "\n\nOrder summary for customer " <<
custName << " \n";
    int i;
    order * x;
    cout << "\n Order = " << (x = orderPtr)-
>orderNum;
    for(i=0;i<orderCount-1;i++) {
      x = x->nextOrder;
      cout << "\n Order = " << x->orderNum;
    };
    return 0;
};
```

It now becomes easier to write logical pointers to maintain the relationships, and parallel the pointer navigation with logical pointers. In other words, we will have two set of pointers; one to navigate the in-memory objects and logical pointers for the objects that only exist in the relational tables.

STEP 5:   Allocate relational tables.

A review of the object structures leads us to the following table declarations. These tables are identical to any other relational implementation except for the absence of foreign keys. These tables also contain fields for the logical pointers that are used by the C++ application to navigate the objects.

Note that each of these tables has a primary key. This key will be generated from the C++ application, and used not only as the primary key for the row, but as a "logical pointer" to establish relationships between objects. Thus, there are no foreign key definitions in these table definitions since all of the object navigation will be handled by the C++ system.

```
Create table CUSTOMER
    (custKey        NUMBER
        CONSTRAINT pk_custKey PRIMARY KEY
        CONSTRAINT nn_custKey NOT NULL,
    custName        CHAR(40),
    firstOrderKey   NUMBER);
```

```
Create table ORDER
    (orderKey              NUMBER
        CONSTRAINT pk_orderKey PRIMARY KEY
        CONSTRAINT nn_orderKey NOT NULL,
    orderNum               NUMBER,
    firstOrderItemKey      NUMBER,
    ownerCustKey           NUMBER,
    nextOrderKey           NUMBER);

Create table ORDERLINE
    (orderlineKey          NUMBER,
    quantity NUMBER,
    nextOrderItemKey       NUMBER,
    nextItemOrderKey       NUMBER,
    ownerOrderKey          NUMBER,
    ownerItemKey           NUMBER);

Create table ITEM
    (itemKey               NUMBER
        CONSTRAINT pk_itemKey PRIMARY KEY
        CONSTRAINT nn_itemKey NOT NULL,
    itemName               CHAR(40),
    firstItemOrderKey      NUMBER,
    firstHasPartKey        NUMBER,
    firstIsAPartKey        NUMBER);

Create table COMPONENT
    (compKey               NUMBER,
    quantity               NUMBER,
    nextHasPartKey         NUMBER,
    nextIsAPartKey         NUMBER);
```

Now that these tables are defined, we can proceed to write the SQL to insert the objects into the tables.

STEP 6: Write C/SQL snippets to move the object data and pointers into the table row.

The final step is to write some code snippets in C that are inserted or linked at the appropriate places in the C++ application. These code snippets will handle all I/O against the relational database. It is worth noting that there is a mismatch between record-at-a-time I/O with object, and the set-at-a-time I/O that we find in a relational database. We will need to review the mapping between these I/O methods to determine how the relational database will map to the C++ application.

In SQL we find several basic I/O operators:

SelectThe SQL SELECT statement returns a set of rows from a table.
InsertThe INSERT statement adds a row to a table.
UpdateThe UPDATE verb changes existing row information.
DeleteThe DELETE operator removes rows from tables.
JoinCannot be used in this method.

With C++, we may find many permutations of pointer manipulation. Object addresses may be captured easily (with the "this" operator) and stored in an array of pointers or in a single CHAR * field. These pointers, in turn, are used by the application to handle all navigation. The following equivalents between C++ and SQL apply:

```
SQL        C++
INSERT     new
DELETE     ~object
SELECT     &object
```

Note that some SQL operators have no direct equivalent in C++. For example, the DELETE operator in SQL can be used to delete many rows from a table (i.e., DELETE FROM tablename WHERE job_title = "manager"). This single SQL statement may have the effect of deleting dozens of rows from the table. In C++ however, the object destructor must be called explicitly each time that an object is destroyed.

Declarative access vs. navigation of objects is also an issue. In SQL, a single SQL statement may update many rows from a table. For example, the SQL UPDATE tablename SET salary = salary*2 WHERE job_title = "manager" may update many rows from the relational table. With a C++ application, I/O is accomplished one object at a time and a loop must be created to update the list of objects.

STEP 7:   Add additional methods to handle object I/O with logical pointers

The final step is to parallel the pointer-based object navigation with another set of methods that allows the objects to be read-from and written-to disk storage. This parallel navigation will use the logical pointers to serve as primary keys in the table definitions. Each constructor will be altered to contain a SQL call to insert the object data into a table:

```
class customer {

  public:
    . . .
    customer(char * p) {     // constructor for
            customer
      firstOrderKey = NULL;

      // access global variable and increment
      int custKey; custtKey = nextCustKey++;

      // convert the pointer to char to a character
      char namefield[81]; strcpy(namefield,
            custName);

      EXEC SQL;
        INSERT INTO CUSTOMER VALUES
          (custKey, namefield, firstOrderKey)
        COMMIT
      END-EXEC;
    };
  };


class order {

  public:
    . . .
    order(customer &cust, int ordnum) {   // order
            constructor
      . . .
      // access global primary key variable and
            increment
      int orderKey; orderKey = nextOrderKey++;
```

```
// Insert the row into the ORDER table
EXEC SQL;
  INSERT INTO ORDER VALUES
  (orderKey, ordernum, custKey,
       logicalNextOrder, firstOrderline)
  COMMIT
END-EXEC;


// Now, update the logical pointer in the
       customer object...
EXEC SQL;
  UPDATE CUSTOMER SET firstOrderKey = orderKey
    WHERE custKey = myKey
  COMMIT
END-EXEC;
};
```

Note that the SQL calls are embedded directly into the C++ application. Most database systems offer pre-compilers for C programs that allow SQL to be embedded within the C programs, and these pre-compilers also will work within a C++ program. A pre-compiler pre-scans the program looking for SQL statements.

When a SQL statement is located, the SQL call is commented-out and replaced with a native C call to the database. Many shops who do not own a C++ compiler for UNIX choose to use freeware versions of C++ compilers, such as the Gnu++ (G++) compiler.

As we see, the insertion of the rows now takes place at the same time that the object is instantiated to the runtime system. Since the objects will continue to exist in memory until the application terminates or the objects are destroyed, there is some question whether it is worthwhile to perform I/O against the database if the object already exists in memory. As the object constructor is invoked we will store the object as a row, but we will never need to issue any SQL SELECTS against this object as long as the object continues to exist in memory. It is always easier to reference objects in-memory than it is to go to the database for them. The question arises when we attempt to retrieve an object that exists to the database (from a prior session) but is unknown to the runtime C++ application. A method needs to be devised to insure that these objects are retrieved in their proper condition.

Writing Object Retrieval

When we look at writing a relational interface to a C++ application we need to address the method to use for getting objects from the relational database. Essentially, the retrieval process is very straightforward. It includes:

1. See if the object is in memory with a physical address.
2. If the object is not in memory retrieve the object with a logical pointer.

The logical pointer was created for the purpose of establishing a primary key for the table. The logical pointer was created when the object was stored into the relational database, and it will be used to navigate between orders.

In our example, we have a method called ordersForCustomers that accepts a "customer" object address and displays the orders for that customer. The logical pointer is called orderKey and it is the primary key for our order table. The code is:

```
customer::ordersForCustomer() {    // list all
              orders  for  a  customer

    cout << "\n\nOrder  summary  for  customer  "  <<
              custName << "  \n";
    int i;
    order * x;
    cout << "\n Order = "  <<  (x = orderPtr)->orderNum;
    for(i=0;i<orderCount-1;i++)  {
      x = x->nextOrder;
      cout << "\n Order = "  <<  x->orderNum;
    };
    return 0;
};
```

Since this is a method of the customer class we already have "currency" on the customer object and we assume that the "customer" object is already in memory. We can see from the code example that the first "order" object is retrieved by checking the orderPtr in the customer object. From the first order, subsequent orders are retrieved by chasing the nextOrder pointer within the order objects.

If we were to write this retrieval IN SQL, the query might look like this:

```
SELECT      orderNum
FROM        order
WHERE       order.custName = "IBM";
```

Of course, this retrieval would return many rows from the order table, and if this query were embedded into a C program, a cursor would need to be declared to fetch each row, one at a time.

```
EXEC SQL   declare c1 cursor for
SELECT      orderNum
FROM        order o
WHERE       order.custName = :custname;

EXEC SQL   open c1;

EXEC SQL   fetch c1 into :orddate;
while (sqlca.sqlcode == 0)
{
   EXEC SQL fetch c1 into :ordnum;
}

EXEC SQL   close c1;
```

We can now look at how these two retrieval methods can be combined into a single C++ routine:

```
customer::ordersForCustomer() {      // list all
            orders for a customer

   cout << "\n\nOrder summary for customer " <<
            custName << " \n";
   int i;
   order * x;

   if (orderPtr == NULL) getOrder(); // if order not
               in memory, fetch RDBMS
   else
     cout << "\n Order =
           " << (x = orderPtr)->orderNum;
                                     // get via addr
```

```
for(i=0;i<orderCount-1;i++)  {
if  (nextOrder  ==  NULL)  getOrder();  //  get  object
          from  RDBMS
else  {  //  if
already  in-memory,
x  =  x->nextOrder;  //  chase  physical  address
cout  <<  "\n  Order  =  "  <<  x->orderNum;
}
};
return  0;
};

getOrder()  {
//  fetch  the  desired  object  from  the  RDBMS...
EXEC  SQL  SELECT  *  from  order  into  :orderstruct
where  orderKey  =  order.orderKey;

//call  the  object  constructor...
order  o123(IBM,:orderNum);
//  Note  that  the  ORDER  constructor  establishes  the
          in-memory
//  pointers  to  the  customer  object  and  related  order
          objects
}
```

The basic premise here is that the in-memory pointers are only established after the object has been retrieved from the RDBMS, and the in-memory pointers have been created by the object constructor.

Note that we first check to see if the object is in memory with the NULL test. If the in memory pointer is NULL, we then call the getOrder() function to retrieve the object from the relational database, calling the object constructor to instantiate the object to the run-time system. The constructor will make the object exist in memory, and establish all necessary pointers to owner objects; i.e., those that already exist in memory. Other pointers to objects that have not yet been retrieved from the relational database will have NULL pointers.

In summary, the paradigms of object-oriented programming and relational databases technology are not as far apart as they appear. If a C++ application is designed with well isolated I/O functions and linked-list navigation, it can be very simple to back-end the C++ application to utilize a relational database.

11

Summary and Future Trends

Let's begin our discussion of future technology with a look into the crystal ball to see how information technology is going to change the way information systems professionals will do business into the next century. It's easy to get caught up in some of the techno-babble relating to future technology. I'm sure all of you are familiar with Alvin Toffler's book, *Future Shock*, in which he discusses how computers are moving out of the machine room and touching how people do their things in everyday life. There is also an excellent book by Nicholas Necroponte, of MIT's Media Lab, *Being Digital*. This book discusses how digital technology is going to enter just about every aspect of our lives, not just what we are accustomed to within the role of information technology. In the book *3001*, Arthur C. Clark observes that the future is not just more than we imagine; it's more than we absolutely can imagine. This is a very exciting time to be in the world of information processing because of the kinds of advances that we have been seeing especially with hardware.

If we start putting things in historical perspective, technology can be viewed as an evolutionary process. One of the things that has been borne out, almost without fail, is that advances in hardware technology necessarily precede advances in the software technology. For example, when Seymour Cray introduced the first Cray Supercomputers, virtually the only customer for supercomputers was the Federal Government: Los Alamos National Laboratories bought one and Lawrence Livermore Labs bought one, but it wasn't until several years later that they were actually able to come up with pragmatic uses for this new supercomputer technology.

Once the industry was able to exploit the features of the technology, companies were able to put the technology to use in the real world. Today, one of the largest markets for supercomputers is in the oil industry, where advanced simulation algorithms are used to predict the probability of striking oil before going out and drilling an expensive well.

As hardware and software costs continue to fall, one of the things that we're going to start seeing is a broadening scope of the kinds of things that information systems shops will be asked to perform. Looking back to when the first IBM mainframes hit the machine room floors in the 1960s, they were generally used to solve very well-structured, mundane, and repetitive tasks—applications such as payroll, personnel management, and other well-structured tasks.

Even today it's surprising to know that 95% of information systems are still caught up in that realm of highly structured, mundane, and repetitive kinds of information processing tasks. The other component of the market, the arena of artificial intelligence and decisions support systems, surprisingly, after the last ten years only consumes about 5% of the total information systems market.

But the marketplace is changing, and in many cases its a change in the perception of the problem domain. As the hardware and software technology becomes more powerful, we're going to see a change in perception according to what kinds of tasks are highly structured and which tasks are considered semi-structured tasks. Remember, a semi-structured task is a task that requires human intuition in order to solve the problem. This distinction is the central difference between expert systems and decision-support systems, whereas an expert system makes a management decision, in and of its own behalf (Figure 11.1).

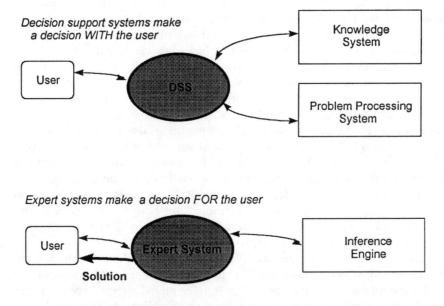

Figure 11.1   Expert systems and decision support systems

A good example of an expert system would be a point-of-sale system in a commercial retail store department. Whenever you buy something in a large retail store, they're actually computing economic order quantity and taking a look at the velocity that the items are going out. The algorithms are aware of how long it takes to get these goods in and the cost of holding them in inventory. All of this is thrown into a highly complex, albeit well-structured model, and the manager is given a report at the end of the day saying this is what you need to reorder and this is how many of them you need to reorder—essentially, a management decision, done without the manager's direct input.

On the other hand, we see the realm of decision-support systems, which are systems that are designed for end-users who rely on their own human intuition to solve the problem (Figure 11.2). Most of the top-level executive managers are in their positions primarily because of their ability to apply human intuition to the real world. We're not going to see computers, at least not in the in near foreseeable future, that will be able to replicate the decision processes of people like Lee Iacocca of Chrysler and other executives earning $80 to $100 million a year. These executives can command these salaries because they are a limited quantity and their problem domain is within the bastion of what we tend to call human intuition.

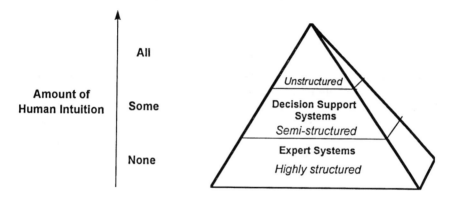

Figure 11.2 A problem domain hierarchy

However, a lot of what is considered to be human intuition is being found, with the advances in technology, to be well-structured. A good example of a decisions-support system would be a system that helps a stock brokerage choose a stock portfolio. For example, anyone who's earned a M.B.A. has learned all the intricacies of stocks. They know about stock betas, covariance analysis, multivariate statistics, and calculus. Every M.B.A. has the same battery of well-structured tools; however, its evident in the marketplace that some people are better at being stock brokers than others. And again, we've entered the realm of human intuition.

Today, information systems can assist these people by helping them deal with the structured component of the problem. A decisions-support system might, for example, set up a model for them where they can set up hypotheses: "What if I bought 10% more of this stock? What if stocks in this arena went up by a factor of 2% per year? What would this do to my model portfolio?" That the DSS spits out an answer and that in turn feeds yet another question into the decision-making process. These are the kinds of things that we're using advanced information systems for today. We're recognizing that human intuition is not quantifiable, and we're not really trying to address it directly.

A good example of how the bar is being raised on problem structure is by examining corporate America. Several years ago, a major canned soup company had a fellow in charge of their tricky soup vats. He had been with the company for 35 years and was getting ready to retire. The company hired some knowledge engineers to come in and capture his decision-making processes. They fully expected that they were going to be building a DSS because everyone on the floor remarked that this man had tremendous intuition. When the knowledge engineers had observed the operation for about three weeks, they were very surprised to discover that they weren't dealing with a decision support system at all. Once they were able to tease out all of the rules that this fellow had used, they found that they were really dealing with a very highly structured, albeit very complex, decision task. It turns out that this gentleman, even though he thought he was using human intuition when workers would come up to him and say, "you know, vat 3 is boiling over, what do I do?" And he just has a feeling, "I have a feeling this is what you do." The person runs off, performs the task, and fixes the problem, all the while being overwhelmed with this man's intuition.

In reality, this man had encountered the same problem twenty years earlier. He couldn't actually remember the exact circumstances, but its these hints, these hunches, these bits of human intuition, that lead people to automatically dismiss some systems as being too advanced to automate. We see the same thing in the marketplace today. If you look at advanced systems for weather forecasting, those that are using the Cray supercomputers, there's an entire area of science called the science of chaos, where they're talking about these phenomenally complex systems being inherently random in nature and therefore, we can't come up with well-structured rules so it's going to be exclusively the domain of human intuition.

It gets back to the old analogy of the butterfly flapping its wings in the Amazon Basin setting off a chain of events that eventually affects North American weather patterns. The analogy I like to give has to do with the changing of perception as to what is a well-structured as opposed to a semi-structured problem. If you take a look at children, they like to play tic-tac-toe and they will spend many hours engrossed in the challenge of this game. After spending all of this time playing the game as children, why don't adults come home after a hard day's work, throw off their coat, and play tic-tac-toe with their spouse? It might seem like a facetious question, but think about it. Has the game of tic-tac-toe changed? No! Our perception of the game has changed.

What to an eight-year old is perceived as a semi-structured problem that requires human intuition and skill, when that child hits the preteens, and abstract thinking kicks in, they recognize tic-tac-toe for what it is, a very well-structured kind of game. All of the challenge and skill is then lost and people stop playing the game.

This is the same kind of thing we're seeing in information systems today. The bar is being raised. It's going to broaden the kinds of information systems that we do. Anyone who lives within the bastion of well-structured thinking, and I'm not excluding computer programmers or database administrators, all of these people tend to work with undeniably well-structured kinds of problems. They're phenomenally complex, but well-structured nonetheless. And these are the kinds of things we do in information systems.

If we look at the future economic benefits from information systems, we all must candidly admit that our job is to displace people who perform well-structured tasks. Every information system since the 1950s has had the primary goal of replacing human resources, hasn't it? That is what information systems are designed to do.

How is this trend towards more advanced well-structured systems going to affect the information systems professional? One of the things we see directly on the horizon is the declining cost of disk storage. In the not so distant past, an IBM 3390 disk with 2 gigabytes of memory cost over $100,000. Today, you can buy a 2.3 gigabyte disk drive for less than $150.

Because of these declining prices, we're now seeing a new age of data warehousing. Even the most conservative companies are now willing to fork out the money it takes to load terabytes of information, so that they can exploit there own data resources. That again, poses challenges. And it gets back to my central premise here that the changes in the hardware technology will precede the changes in the software technology.

Today we're seeing people building humongous data warehouses of trillions and trillions of bytes, and people don't really have a clue how they're going to use them. Even the vendor communities don't have any idea how to serve this exploding marketplace. You've got your basic ad-hoc queries in a data warehouse, but people are looking for more advanced modeling hypothesis testing capabilities. Vendors are springing up right and left offering these data mining tools that are based on artificial intelligence, with all kinds of great buzz words like neural networks and fuzzy logic and all kinds of phenomenally complex things that are going to allow us to mine our data information resources and make better use of unobtrusive data trends that lie within our data warehouse.

These are the kinds of things we can look forward to in just the next couple of years. We're also seeing the same thing happen in the realm of real memory. As RAM memory continues to get cheaper, we're entering an age called VLM (very large memory). In some cases, organizations run Oracle databases with memory regions in excess of half a gigabyte. When they start up the system in the morning, the database performs an area sweep of the whole database, sucking it all in into memory, and the database remains within RAM memory all day with blistering response time.

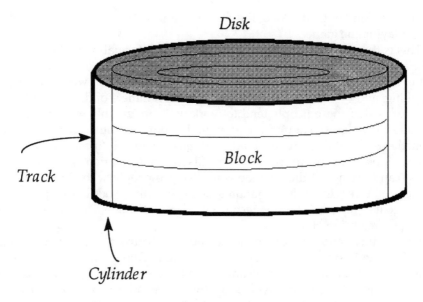

Figure 11.3   A Direct Access Storage Device (DASD)

Take a look at what's going on with the new 64-bit technology on midrange processors. They offer blistering performance improvements over earlier releases. In recent studies, SQL queries that ran for an hour using 32 bit technology take less than half a second to run on a 64-bit machine with very large memory configurations.

What the industry is seeing is an exponentially improving response time and performance of most kinds of information systems. You may recall when the supercomputer machines first came out, a lot of people criticized them and wondered what benefit there would be to finishing an eight-hour batch window in ten minutes. But, it wasn't until people actually got this technology and began to use it, that we began to see changes in the way we did business within information systems. Some of the things we're going to start seeing with this new advent of cheaper SIMS chips, is a complete movement away from disk as a storage media.

Devices such as the IBM 3390 mainframe disks are going to be relegated to the computer museum in the very near future. If we take a look at the access time differences between RAM chips and disk, disk is more than 10,000 times slower. Think about disk technology. We're using a technology that has not changed a whole lot in 25 years (Figure 11.3).

But, we're going to start seeing these improvements in very large memory and they're going to be impacting all areas of information systems. Many industry analysts believe that within the next ten years, keyboards are going to be as archaic as punched cards.

Automatic Speech Recognition

Often, a new technology is driven by necessity. For example, a quadriplegic programmer has developed an automatic speech recognition system entirely out of necessity because he does not have the use of his hands, and the only thing holding him back from making commercially available products was the high cost of RAM memory. At the time it required about a hundred megabytes of memory, but now he's got what they call continuous speech recognition capability with 200 Mb of RAM, which is still expensive for today's PC's, but is certainly not out of reach for many different kinds of applications.

This product has become a commercial product favored by physicians and attorneys. They can directly dictate their information onto the computer without having people transcribe that kind of information. So again, within the marketplace, clerical skills as we know them are disappearing. Just as in the last twenty years nobody learns Gregg shorthand in secretarial school anymore because it's been displaced by tape recorders, so too, keyboarding will become obsolete.

A lot of the new technology has been driven by the U. S. Government. Automatic speech recognition (ASR) had its start with the CIA doing research for the Northwest Parallel Computing Resource Center in Syracuse, New York. The government has been working on databases where a user can make an English query into a Russian database and return the results said in French. These kinds of dynamic language translations are of immense value but they didn't come without a cost. In the 1980s, IBM spent years and millions of dollars learning how to parse spoken English with a computer. For example, it is very difficult for a computer to understand that the word "bus station" is two words and not one, since they are pronounced as a single sound.

But parsing out the spoken words is just the beginning. Once you've parsed the word, you still have to be able to derive meaning from that spoken word, and that's a very difficult challenge in and of itself, especially because of the natural ambiguities that come out of the human language. Just a simple phrase, like "Mary had a little lamb," causes confusion in a computer. It can't resolve the verb "had" in the sentence. The computer would ask, "What do you mean by Mary had a little lamb? Did Mary buy a little lamb? Did Mary eat a little lamb? Do we take a biblical interpretation of "had"? What do you mean Mary "had" a little lamb?"

These kinds of natural ambiguities occur in spoken English all the time and it's very difficult to get computers to resolve the nuances of the English language. For example, there was a product in the 1970s marketed by Excalibur Corporation called Savvy, which was a natural language interface to databases. It worked for very simple queries, but when you gave it something sophisticated, or ambiguous like "How long has Joe been with us?" Savvy would come back and say, "What are you asking for, Joe's date of birth or Joe's date of hire?"

See, so you have these kinds of natural ambiguities that have to be addressed, and the language translation routines often produce hilarious results. Consider the phrase, "The spirit is willing, but the flesh is weak." Translated into Russian, and then translated back into English it read "the vodka is good, but the meat is rotten." Hardly a literal translation of that phrase.

But this type of technology is getting much more sophisticated and we are actually going to start seeing ASR, the whole area of Automatic Speech Recognition, taking over the desktops. We will actually be keyboard and mouse free, and people will actually interact with their computers, much as they would if they were individuals today. Within the more mundane realm of information systems, we're finally seeing another nascent technology finally taking off. And here, we're talking about object technology.

The Future of Object Technology

About three years ago, the major industries recognized that object technology with its objects, classes, behaviors, and messages has a lot to bring to the table. You have the ability to provide polymorphism, encapsulation, and inheritance and all these other new terms and words that nobody understands, but have very compelling reasons to be there.

Larry Ellison, the other billionaire, announced that his Oracle database was going to have object-oriented features. In fact, Oracle8, they're calling it Oracle "late" because of delays in the delivery of the product spanning nearly four years, does indeed support many of the object technology constructs, like pointers and inheritance and the ability to define class libraries. It's going to turn the entire data processing world on its side.

As we may know, Michael Stonebreaker's famous Illustra database, the object oriented database that used data blades, was recently purchased by Informix Corporation. Informix is rearchitecting Informix from the ground up to be a robust object oriented database, and it will soon become a major player in the object/relational database market. So, we're starting to see a major change, not only in the kinds of systems that we develop, the sorts of applications that we support, but in the technology that is actually driving these kinds of applications.

As we broaden our base of technology, and push the limit of well-structured kinds of systems to a higher plane, a whole different kind of occupation is going to be coming up for IT resources. For example, within the mundane realm of database administration, computer programming is going to change radically. It is referred to as the programming revolution, which will begin in

1998 as these databases make their way into the mainstream, it's analogous to the Industrial Revolution of the 18th century. Prior to the Industrial Revolution, people were individual craftsmen. Each and every rifle was it's own unique work of art. After the Industrial Revolution, the jobs of gun makers changed. Rather than being custom craftsmen, they became assemblers of pre-manufactured components. That very same thing is going to be happening to the jobs of applications programmers today and it's being largely driven by the major hardware and software vendors.

Changes in systems development is going to become radically different, but it's not going to happen overnight. Programmers have recognized that creating these reusable capsules of code can dramatically change and improve the way that information systems are developed. For example, the programmer of the future isn't going to write that much custom code. They're simply going to be assembling from prewritten, pretested components. And the benefits of this type of system development should be self-evident, and what you will see is that all the SQL, all the application process codes move out of the application and move into these object oriented databases, where its tightly coupled with the objects.

The OMGs CORBA (Common Object Request Broker Architecture) and Microsoft's DCOM (Distributed Common Object Model) are taking over as the de facto standards for interoperable systems communication. These emerging standards are what is driving our industry today and are going to have a profound impact on the way we, as IT professionals, do business. With all of the process code moving out of applications programs and into the database, it opens up entire new job opportunities, especially in the Information processing professions.

The computer industry can be very fickle. The IT industry has a fantastic rate of change that is broadening the scope of the way information systems are handled and managed. We're going to start seeing the whole era of Very Large Memory Systems. Just look at the last ten years, and see how things have changed. For example, look at normalization that is used in database design. You learn to tear things apart, and put them in their most atomic, tiny pieces, because you don't want to have redundancy. Redundancy was always considered bad. Well, that changed as disk prices fell. It was almost as if one morning the industry woke up and said, "Hey, guess what? Now, redundancy is good!" But wait a minute, it was bad yesterday. "No, it's good, now."

And that's what we see in this whole computer arena, we're finding that the rules are changing, like the attitudes towards data redundancy. For example, you'll notice all of the major databases are supporting a synchronous replication, snapshots, mirrored databases, and Redundant Arrays of Inexpensive Disk (RAID). So again, we're seeing more examples of how the changes in these hardware arenas are influencing the way we do business in information systems. It also has a tremendous impact on the way information systems are designed.

Software products of the future are also going to change in their fundamental nature. For example, database products aren't going to have roll forward capability anymore. It takes a tremendous amount of database resources to write the before and after images of every record that has been updated in an OLTP environment. The only reason the legacy databases write these images is in case you have a disk crash and you have to roll the database forward to a point in time prior to the disk failure. But doesn't that become a moot issue with RAID technology? With RAID, you have continuous 7 / 24 support; if a disk goes bad, you run over, unplug it, slap in another disk, it resynchronizes, and there is never any system unavailability due to disk failure. Hence, we're seeing the reaction of the software community to the advances in hardware technology. The major software vendors react to the change in hardware technology, and it cascades on down to where we are today.

Summary

We are beginning to see changes in the roles of everyone who works with computers—the roles of computer programmers are going to radically change into the roles of code assemblers; the roles of the systems analysts are going to become much broader with the advent of object technology. Class hierarchies, polymorphism, encapsulation, all of these wild and wonderful tools are going to present challenges to the systems development community. Now is the time to gear up for it. If you are considering sitting in your ivory tower, hoping it'll go away, you're going to be in for a surprise. The major software vendors are forcing us to embrace these new ways of doing things and now is the time to prepare for them.

Appendix A
Original C++ Application

```cpp
#include <iostream.h>
#include <string.h>
#include <math.h>
#include <stdlib.h>
#include <time.h>

class customer;
class order;
class orderline;
class item;
class component;

class customer {
  public:
    char * custName;
    order ** orderList;              // pointers to
              orders for this customer
    int orderCount;
    customer(char * p) {             // constructor for
              customer
      cout << "creating customer " << p << "\n";
      int l;
      l = strlen(p);                 //  get length of
              string
      custName = new char[l+1];      // get space for
              customer name
      if (!custName) { cout << "allocation error!\n";
              exit(1);}
      strcpy(custName,p);            // copy in the
              customer name
      orderCount = 0;
    };
```

213

```
    ordersForCustomer() {              // list all orders
                for a customer

      cout << "\n\nOrder summary for customer " <<
              custName <<" \n";
      int i;
      for(i=0;i<orderCount;i++) {
        cout <<  "\n   Order = " << orderList[i]->
              orderNum;
      };
      return 0;
    };
  };

class order {

  public:
    customer * custOwner;             // pointer to
                customer placing this order
    orderline ** itemList;            // pointers to line
                items in the order
    int orderNum, itemCount;

    order(customer &cust, int ordnum)    {
                                      // order constructor
      cout << "\nCreating order " << ordnum << "\n";
      itemCount = 0;
      orderNum = ordnum;              // set the order
                number
      cust.orderList[cust.orderCount++] = this;
                                      // set cust -> order
      custOwner = &cust;              // set order->
                customer pointer
    };
    itemsInOrder()  { //   {          // list all items for
                an order
      // get the items and count the item names...
      cout << "\n\n Item list for order number " <<
              orderNum << "\n";
      int i, quant;
```

```
      float pr, totCost;
      for(i=0;i<itemCount;i++) {
        // get the orderline object ...
        item * temp = itemList[i]->itemOwner;
        // get the item object ...
        pr = temp->itemPrice;
        // save the quantity ordered
        quant = itemList[i]->quantity;
        totCost = pr * quant;
        cout << "   Item " << temp->itemName;
        cout << " cost "   << pr;
        cout << " quant "  << quant;
        cout << " total "  << totCost << "\n";
      };
      return 0;
    };

  };


class item {

  public:
    orderline ** orderList;          // pointers to
                 orderlines
    component ** hasParts;           // pointers to
                 has-parts
    component ** isAPart;            // pointers to
                 is-a-part
    char * itemName;
    int inventoryLevel, price, orderCount, hasPartCount,
             isAPartCount;
    float itemPrice;

    item(char * p, int quantityReceived, float price ) {
                                     // item constructor

      cout << "\nCreating item " << p << "\n";
      orderCount=0;
      itemPrice = price;             // set item price;
```

```
        inventoryLevel = quantityReceived;
                                        // set quantity
        int l;
        l = strlen(p);                  // get length of
                string

        itemName = new char[l+1];       // get space for name
        if (!itemName) { cout << "allocation error!\n";
                exit(1);}
        strcpy(itemName,p);             // copy in item name

    };
  };

class orderline {

  public:
    order * orderOwner;                 // pointer to order
    item  * itemOwner;                  // pointer to item
    int quantity;
    orderline(order &ord, item &it, int qty) {
                                        // orderline
            constructor

      cout << "     creating orderline\n";
      ord.itemList[ord.itemCount++] = this;
                                        // set cust -> order
      it.orderList[it.orderCount++] = this;
      orderOwner = &ord;                // set pointer to
                order
      itemOwner  = &it;                 // set pointer to
                item
      quantity = qty;                   // set quantity
                ordered
    };
  };

class component {

  public:
    item * hasAPart;                        // pointer to owner
```

```
                item
   item * isAPart;                        // pointer to owner
                item
   int quantity;
   component(item &has, item  &isA, int quant) {
                                          // BOM constructor
     has.hasParts[has.hasPartCount++] = this;
                                          // set has-part
                pointer
     isA.isAPart[isA.isAPartCount++]  = this;
                                          // set is-a-part
     quantity = quant;                    // set quantity
   }
 };

main() {

customer IBM("IBM");
customer ATnT("ATnT");

item pen("pen",300,1.95);
item pencil("pencil",400,1.30);
item pad("pad",100,2.95);

order o123(IBM,123);
  orderline i1(o123,pen,3);
  orderline i2(o123,pencil,4);

order o456(ATnT,456);
  orderline i3(o456,pen,6);
  orderline i4(o456,pencil,16);
  orderline i5(o456,pad,12);

order o789(ATnT,789);
  orderline i6(o789,pencil,50);
  orderline i7(o789,pad,10);
  orderline i8(o789,pen,2);

IBM.ordersForCustomer();

ATnT.ordersForCustomer();
```

```
o123.itemsInOrder();

o456.itemsInOrder();

o789.itemsInOrder();

//ATnT.ordersForCustomer();
//IBM.ordersForCustomer();

return 0;

}
```

Index